Betty Crocker's
SOUPS
AND STEWS

PRENTICE HALL

New York   London   Toronto   Sydney   Tokyo   Singapore

PRENTICE HALL GENERAL REFERENCE
15 Columbus Circle
New York, New York 10023

Library of Congress Cataloging-in-Publication Data

Crocker, Betty.
    [Soups and stews]
    Betty Crocker's soups and stews.
       p.   cm.
    Includes index.
    ISBN 0-671-86960-4
    1. Stews. I. Title. II. Title: Soups and stews.
    TX693.C765 1994
    641.8'13—dc20   92-44793
                                                CIP

Designed by Carla Weise/Levavi & Levavi, Inc.

Manufactured in the United States of America

        10 9 8 7 6 5 4 3 2 1

First Edition

Front cover: Zuni Vegetable Stew (page 60)

Back cover: Bouillabaisse (page 57)

Contents

Letter from the Editors

Soups and stews are cozy and friendly, offering warmth and heartiness in the winter months; in warm weather, cold soups are a welcome, refreshing meal. Soups and stews can be a complete meal, serve as a tasty accompaniment to a sandwich, or be the first course of a more formal meal. In fact, there almost always seems to be a place for soups and stews on everyone's menu, and you'll find all the best right here.

Enjoy hearty Beef Provencale, and Hungarian Beef Goulash; if you prefer chicken, you'll love our classic Chicken and Dumplings or Chicken Noodle Soup. Seafood lovers will enjoy both Manhattan and New England Clam Chower, as well as Shrimp Gumbo and Bouillabaisse.

And when you'd like a meatless soup or stew, sample zesty Zuni Vegetable Stew, Golden Onion Soup or Minestrone with Pesto. What can you do when it feels too hot to eat? Serve up soup! Our chapter on cold soups will tempt the appetite on the most sweltering days. Try cold raspberry Soup, Gazpacho or Cold Yogurt-Cucumber Soup for a sure-fire meal.

Whether you are looking for a main dish, a side dish, or just great taste, you'll find just what you are looking for in BETTY CROCKER'S SOUPS AND STEWS.

The Betty Crocker Editors

Introduction

While we love soups and stews, sometimes it's hard to find the time to make a long-simmering dish. Below you'll find options and suggestions that allow you to enjoy soups and stews, even when your schedule is hectic.

SOUPS ON THE RUN

Follow these tips to make meals away from home delicious and safe. Remember, food that has been kept too long at room temperature can be a health hazard, so always refrigerate your soup or stew until it's time to eat.

- Cook up a big pot of soup or stew on the weekend and bring a serving of it for lunch during the week. Soup can be kept in the refrigerator for 2 to 3 days.
- Put soup in a leakproof and microwavable container and refrigerate until serving time. Microwave it to reheat. Brothlike soups reheat especially well in the microwave because they heat quickly and evenly without separating.

FREEZING SOUPS AND STEWS

Soup freezes exceptionally well. You can cook up a double recipe of your favorite soup or stew and freeze half. It will save you time, and you'll have a delicious soup waiting for you in the freezer on a day when you don't have the time to make it from scratch.

- Freezing makes potatoes grainy and soft, so leave potatoes out of the soups and stews until it's time to reheat. Be sure to cook the potatoes before you add them to the soup or stew.
- Select a plastic freezer container that holds enough soup for one meal—a quart container holds 4 to 6 servings and a pint container holds 2 to 3 servings.
- Use containers with wide openings so soup can be easily removed when only partially thawed.
- Leave ½-inch headspace in quart containers and ¼-inch headspace in pint containers because liquids expand when frozen.
- Label each container with the soup name, number of servings and date you froze it.
- Soups and stews keep well in the freezer for 2 to 3 months.
- Thaw frozen soups in the refrigerator.
- Be sure to use fully thawed soups immediately.
- Although some flavors intensify in the freezing process, onion gradually loses its flavor. Season to taste after reheating.

SOUP SHORTCUTS

You don't always have time to whip up your own chicken or beef broth. Canned soups and broths are certainly delicious and convenient substitutes. Here are some ideas on how to cut down on preparation time without cutting down on flavor.

- To make broth from bouillon: For each cup of broth, simply dissolve 1 bouillon cube or 1 teaspoon instant bouillon in 1 cup of boiling water.
- Make an impromptu soup by adding leftover, cooked vegetables to broth or bouillon. Add your favorite spices and some croutons or crackers for garnish, and you have a delicious soup in no time.
- Salad bars in delis and groceries can be a boon to the chef in a hurry. If you don't have time to chop and peel vegetables for soup, you can pick up already prepared vegetables in many stores.

CANNED COMBINATIONS

Canned soups can be a quick way to make a satisfying meal. Try some of the soup combinations below for a new twist on your old favorites. You'll enjoy the new flavors, and may even be inspired to create your own combinations.

CONDENSED SOUP 1 CAN EACH	LIQUID	ADDITION	SERVINGS
Bean with Bacon (11 ounces)	2 soup cans water		5 servings (1 cup each)
Vegetable (10½ ounces)			
Cheddar Cheese (11 ounces)	1 soup can water, 1 soup can milk		5 servings (1 cup each)
Split Pea with Ham and Bacon (11½ ounces)			
Chicken Noodle (10¾ ounces)	2 soup cans water		5 servings (1 cup each)
French Onion (10½ ounces)			
Cream of Chicken (10¾ ounces)	1 soup can water	¼ teaspoon curry powder	3 servings (about ¾ cup each)
Tomato (10¾ ounces)	1 soup can milk	¼ teaspoon ground cloves	3 servings (about ¾ cup each)
Tomato (10¾ ounces)	1 soup can water, 1 soup can milk		5 servings (1 cup each)
Beef Noodle (10¾ ounces)			
Tomato (10¾ ounces)	1 soup can water, 1 soup can milk		5 servings (1 cup each)
Chicken Gumbo (10¾ ounces)			

BETTER WITH BREAD

Serving bread with soups and stews is always satisfying. Whether you dunk, soak, or sop up liquid, bread adds to the meal. Everyone has their favorite breads, cornbread with chile, crusty French bread with onion soup, crackers with chowder. While we often buy our bread, or use favorite, tried-and-true recipes, it's fun to have a few ideas to "fix up" store bought breads or make croutons.

- Refrigerated or frozen doughs are just right to make your own fresh-from-the-oven bread-sticks. Choose from the variety available to suit the soup or stew you are making.
- Make pita bread or tortillas special. Brush split pita bread or tortillas with melted margarine or butter and sprinkle with herbs. Bake at 400° 6 to 8 minutes.

Garlic Bread

½ cup margarine or butter, softened
1 clove garlic, finely chopped
1 loaf (1 pound) French bread, cut into
   15 slices

Heat oven to 400°. Mix margarine and garlic. Spread over bread slices. Reassemble loaf and wrap securely in heavy-duty aluminum foil. Bake 15 to 20 minutes or until hot.

TO MICROWAVE: Do not wrap loaf in aluminum foil. Divide assembled loaf in half and place halves side by side in napkin-lined basket or on microwavable dinner plate. Cover with microwavable paper towel and microwave on medium (50%) 1 minute 30 seconds to 3 minutes, rotating basket ½ turn after 1 minute, until bread is warm.

HERB-CHEESE BREAD: Add 2 tablespoons grated Parmesan cheese, 2 teaspoons chopped fresh parsley and 1 teaspoon chopped fresh or ½ teaspoon dried oregano leaves to the margarine mixture. **1 loaf (15 slices)**

Croutons

Cut your preferred bread—French, Italian, whole wheat, rye, croissants, etc—into ½ inch slices; spread one side with softened margarine or butter. Cut into ½ inch cubes. Sprinkle with chopped herbs, grated Parmesan cheese or spices, if desired. Place in ungreased, heavy skillet. Cook over medium heat, stirring frequently, 4 to 7 minutes or until golden brown.

HOW TO USE NUTRITION INFORMATION

Nutrition Information per serving for each recipe includes the amounts of calories, protein, carbohydrate, fat, cholesterol and sodium.

- If ingredient choices are given, the first listed ingredient is used in recipe nutrition information calculations.
- When ingredient ranges or more than one serving size is indicated, the first weight or serving is used to calculate nutrition information.
- "If desired" ingredients and recipe variations are not included in nutrition information calculations.

MENUS

REFRESHING LUNCH
Cheese and Crackers
Gazpacho (page 83)
Watermelon Slices
Iced Tea

EASY WEEKDAY DINNER
Hamburger Minestrone (page 8)
Garlic Bread (page vii)
Tossed Green Salad
Sliced Pears and Cookies
Milk

COMPANY DINNER
Shrimp Gumbo (page 55)
Corn Sticks or Corn Bread
Green Salad with Toasted Sunflower Seeds and
Chick Peas
Pralines or Praline Ice Cream with Caramel
  Sauce
Coffee or Tea

SUNDAY DINNER
Chicken and Dumplings (page 30)
Three Bean Salad
Whole Wheat Dinner Rolls
Rice Pudding
Wine or Fruit Juice

CHILI PARTY
Texas Red Chile (page 5)
Chips and Salsa
Sliced Avacado Salad
Pecan Pie
Beer or Seltzer

WEEKEND LUNCH
Lentil and Brown Rice Soup (page 61)
Muffins
Cut-up Vegetables
Brownies
Lemonade or Milk

Beef-Vegetable Stew with Barley (page 2)

1

Meaty Mainstays

■

Beef and Broth

**2 pounds beef shank cross cuts or soup
bones**
6 cups cold water
1 teaspoon salt
¼ teaspoon dried thyme leaves
1 carrot, cut up
1 stalk celery with leaves, cut up
1 small onion, cut up
5 peppercorns
3 whole cloves
3 sprigs parsley
1 bay leaf

Remove marrow from center of bones. Heat
marrow in Dutch oven over low heat until
melted, or heat 2 tablespoons vegetable oil until
hot. Cook beef shanks over medium heat until
brown on both sides. Add water and heat to boiling. Skim foam from broth. Stir in remaining ingredients and heat to boiling. Skim foam from
broth; reduce heat. Cover and simmer 3 hours.
Remove beef from broth. Cool beef about 10
minutes or just until cool enough to handle.
Strain broth through cheesecloth-lined sieve;
discard vegetables and seasonings. Remove
beef from bones. Cut beef into ½-inch pieces.
Skim fat from broth. Cover and refrigerate broth
and beef in separate containers no longer than
24 hours, or freeze for future use.

About 3 cups cooked beef

PER SERVING: Calories 290; Protein 41 g; Carbohydrate 0 g; Fat 13 g; Cholesterol 125 mg; Sodium 100 mg

Beef Stew

This hearty stew is especially welcome on cold, wintery days. And, its easy to pop in the oven, letting you go about your business without a lot of bother.

2 pounds beef stew meat, cut into 1-inch cubes
⅓ cup quick-cooking tapioca
1 tablespoon chopped fresh or 1 teaspoon dried basil leaves
1 tablespoon cumin seed
1 teaspoon salt
4 medium carrots, cut into 1-inch pieces
4 cloves garlic, finely chopped
2 medium onions, cut into eighths
2 cans (16 ounces) tomatoes, undrained
2 ears fresh corn, cut into fourths,* or 1 package (10 ounces) frozen whole kernel corn
8 small new potatoes (about 1 pound), cut in half
2 small zucchini, thinly sliced

Heat oven to 325°. Mix all ingredients except corn, potatoes and zucchini in Dutch oven; break up tomatoes. Cover and bake 2½ hours, stirring 2 or 3 times during the first 1½ hours. Stir corn and potatoes into stew. Cover and bake 1 to 1½ hours longer or until beef and vegetables are tender. Stir in zucchini. Cover and let stand 10 minutes. **8 servings**

4 ears frozen corn, thawed and cut in half, can be substituted for the fresh corn.

PER SERVING: Calories 305; Protein 28 g; Carbohydrate 37 g; Fat 6 g; Cholesterol 70 mg; Sodium 530 mg

Beef-Vegetable Stew with Barley

1 pound beef stew meat, cut into 1-inch pieces
1 tablespoon vegetable oil
1 cup dry red wine or beef broth
1 teaspoon chopped fresh or ¼ teaspoon dried rosemary leaves, crushed
¼ teaspoon pepper
1 clove garlic, finely chopped
1 can (10½ ounces) condensed beef broth
1 can (14½ ounces) whole tomatoes, undrained
½ cup uncooked barley
2 cups sliced carrots (about 2 medium)
1 cup broccoli flowerets
4 ounces medium mushrooms, cut into halves
1 medium onion, cut into wedges

Cook beef in oil in 4-quart Dutch oven, stirring occasionally, until brown. Stir in wine, rosemary, pepper, garlic, broth and tomatoes; break up tomatoes. Heat to boiling; reduce heat. Cover and simmer 1 hour.

Stir in barley. Cover and simmer about 30 minutes or until beef is almost tender. Stir in remaining ingredients. Cover and simmer about 20 minutes or until vegetables are tender.

4 servings

PER SERVING: Calories 290; Protein 23 g; Carbohydrate 23 g; Fat 9 g; Cholesterol 55 mg; Sodium 330 mg

Beef Stew Provençale

Salt pork adds lusty country flavor to a stock seasoned with thyme and rosemary.

¼ pound salt pork
1½ pounds beef boneless chuck, tip or
  round
1 cup dry red wine or beef broth
½ cup water
2 cloves garlic, chopped
½ teaspoon salt
½ teaspoon dried thyme leaves
¼ teaspoon dried rosemary leaves,
  crushed
¼ teaspoon pepper
1 bay leaf
6 medium carrots, cut into 1-inch pieces
2 medium onions, cut into fourths
½ cup pitted ripe olives
Chopped parsley
French bread

Remove rind from salt pork; cut pork into ¼-inch slices. Cut beef into 1-inch cubes. (For ease in cutting, partially freeze beef about 1 hour.) Fry salt pork in Dutch oven over medium heat until crisp; remove with slotted spoon. Drain on paper towels. Cook and stir beef in hot fat until brown, about 15 minutes. Drain fat. Add wine, water, garlic, salt, thyme, rosemary, pepper and bay leaf. Heat to boiling; reduce heat. Cover and simmer 1 hour.

Stir in salt pork, carrots, onions and olives. Cover and simmer until beef and vegetables are tender, about 40 minutes. Remove bay leaf. Sprinkle with parsley. Serve in bowls with French bread for dipping.   **6 servings**

PER SERVING: Calories 600; Protein 32 g; Carbohydrate 26 g; Fat 41 g; Cholesterol 105 mg; Sodium 700 mg

Hungarian Beef Goulash

This dish is the quintessential Hungarian stew, filled with potatoes, beef and tomatoes and seasoned with caraway and paprika.

2 tablespoons vegetable oil or bacon fat
1½ pounds beef boneless chuck, tip or
  round, cut into ¾-inch cubes
2 cups water
1 can (8 ounces) tomatoes (with liquid)
3 medium onions, chopped
1 clove garlic, chopped
2 teaspoons paprika
2 teaspoons salt
1 teaspoon instant beef bouillon
½ teaspoon caraway seed
¼ teaspoon pepper
2 medium potatoes, cut into 1½-inch
  pieces
2 medium green peppers, cut into 1-inch
  pieces
French bread or rolls

Heat oil in Dutch oven or 12-inch skillet until hot. Cook and stir beef in hot oil until brown, about 15 minutes; drain. Add water, tomatoes, onions, garlic, paprika, salt, bouillon, caraway seed and pepper. Break up tomatoes. Heat to boiling; reduce heat. Cover and simmer 1 hour.

Add potatoes; cover and simmer until beef and potatoes are tender, about 30 minutes. Add green peppers; cover and simmer until tender, 8 to 10 minutes. Serve in soup bowls with French bread for dipping into hot broth.

6 servings

PER SERVING: Calories 565; Protein 31 g; Carbohydrate 31 g; Fat 35 g; Cholesterol 95 mg; Sodium 1290 mg

Beef and Onion Stew

This aromatic stew showcases sweet and tender pearl onions. It is a Greek specialty with a tomato base, touched with cinnamon, and is served with a bold feta cheese topping.

1 medium onion, chopped
2 cloves garlic, finely chopped
3 tablespoons olive or vegetable oil
2 pounds beef boneless chuck, tip or round, cut into 1-inch cubes
½ cup dry red wine or beef broth
2 tablespoons red wine vinegar
½ teaspoon salt
¼ teaspoon coarsely ground pepper
1 bay leaf
1 stick cinnamon
1 can (8 ounces) tomato sauce
1½ pounds pearl onions, peeled
Crumbled feta cheese

Cook and stir chopped onion and garlic in oil in Dutch oven over medium heat until onion is tender; remove with slotted spoon. Cook beef in remaining oil, stirring frequently, until all liquid is evaporated and beef is brown on all sides, about 25 minutes; drain fat.

Return onion and garlic to Dutch oven. Stir in remaining ingredients except pearl onions and cheese. Heat to boiling; reduce heat. Cover and simmer 1 hour and 15 minutes.

Add pearl onions. Cover and simmer until beef and pearl onions are tender, about 30 minutes. Remove bay leaf and cinnamon. Garnish with cheese.   **6 servings**

PER SERVING: Calories 475; Protein 43 g; Carbohydrate 16 g; Fat 26 g; Cholesterol 130 mg; Sodium 620 mg

Economy Cuts of Meat

Because most hearty soups and stews simmer for a lengthy period of time, less expensive cuts of meat can be used—and they'll be quite tender when cooked.

- Beef stew meat is usually cut from the boneless chuck or round sections.
- Pork stew meat is usually cut from the Boston shoulder or picnic shoulder sections.
- Lamb stew meat is usually cut from the shoulder or leg sections or from the neck.

Compare the price per pound of these cuts (including the waste) with ready-cut meat. You may find it more economical to cut up the meat yourself.

Beef and Tequila Stew

2 pounds beef boneless chuck, tip or
round, cut into 1-inch cubes
¼ cup all-purpose flour
¼ cup vegetable oil
1 medium onion, chopped (about ½ cup)
2 slices bacon, cut up
¼ cup chopped carrot
¼ cup chopped celery
¼ cup tequila
¾ cup tomato juice
2 tablespoons chopped fresh cilantro
1½ teaspoons salt
1 can (15 ounces) garbanzo beans
4 medium tomatoes, chopped (about 4
cups)
2 cloves garlic, finely chopped

Coat beef with flour. Heat oil in 10-inch skillet until hot. Cook and stir beef in oil over medium heat until brown. Remove beef with slotted spoon and drain. Cook and stir onion and bacon in same skillet until bacon is crisp.

Stir in beef and remaining ingredients. Heat to boiling; reduce heat. Cover and simmer until beef is tender, about 1 hour. **6 servings**

PER SERVING: Calories 715; Protein 42 g; Carbohydrate 22 g; Fat 51 g; Cholesterol 130 mg; Sodium 900 mg

Texas Red Chile

A hearty chile that showcases the different forms of the chile plant.

3 pounds beef boneless round steak, cut
into 1-inch cubes
1 large onion, finely chopped (about 1
cup)
4 cloves garlic, finely chopped
2 cups tomato purée
¼ cup vegetable oil
2 to 3 tablespoons ground red chiles
1 teaspoon cumin seed, ground
1 teaspoon ground coriander
4 Anaheim chiles, seeded and chopped
4 jalapeño chiles, seeded and chopped
Shredded Cheddar cheese
Flour tortillas
Cooked pinto beans

Cook and stir beef, onion and garlic in oil in 4-quart Dutch oven over medium heat until beef is brown. Stir in remaining ingredients except cheese, tortillas and beans.

Heat to boiling; reduce heat. Cover and simmer, stirring occasionally, until beef is tender, about 2 hours. Serve with cheese, tortillas and beans. **6 servings**

PER SERVING: Calories 860; Protein 77 g; Carbohydrate 52 g; Fat 38 g; Cholesterol 185 mg; Sodium 815 mg

Burger Beef Soup

Burger Beef Soup

1 pound ground beef
1 small onion, chopped (about ¼ cup)
2 cups tomato juice
1¼ cups water
½ cup frozen peas
¾ teaspoon chopped fresh or ¼ teaspoon dried basil
¾ teaspoon chopped fresh or ¼ teaspoon dried marjoram
⅛ teaspoon pepper
1 bay leaf
1 can (10¾ ounces) condensed cream of celery soup
2 ounces uncooked egg noodles (1 cup)

Cook ground beef and onion in 4-quart Dutch oven over medium heat about 10 minutes, stirring frequently, or until beef is brown; drain. Stir in remaining ingredients except noodles. Heat to boiling. Stir in noodles; reduce heat. Simmer uncovered about 10 minutes, stirring occasionally, until noodles are tender. Remove bay leaf. **4 servings**

PER SERVING: Calories 385; Protein 23 g; Carbohydrate 24 g; Fat 22 g; Cholesterol 90 mg; Sodium 1100 mg

Sauerkraut-Meatball Soup

A quick, tasty dinner for a busy night.

1 pound ground beef
½ teaspoon caraway seed
½ teaspoon garlic powder
¼ cup ketchup
1 can (14½ ounces) Italian-style stewed tomatoes, undrained
1 can (14½ ounces) beef broth
1 can (8 ounces) sauerkraut, drained

Mix ground beef, caraway seed and garlic powder. Shape mixture into sixteen 1½-inch meatballs. Place in 4-quart Dutch oven. Cook over medium heat until brown; drain. Stir in remaining ingredients. Heat to boiling, stirring occasionally; reduce heat. Cover and simmer 10 minutes, stirring occasionally. **4 servings**

PER SERVING: Calories 300; Protein 22 g; Carbohydrate 12 g; Fat 18 g; Cholesterol 70 mg; Sodium 1080 mg

Meatball Minestrone

Mini Meatballs (below)
1 can (28 ounces) whole tomatoes, undrained
1 can (15 ounces) kidney beans, undrained
1 can (12 ounces) vacuum-packed whole kernel corn, undrained
2 cups water
½ cup dry red wine or water
1 tablespoon Italian seasoning
1 teaspoon salt
½ teaspoon pepper
2 stalks celery, sliced (about 1 cup)
1 medium onion, chopped (about ½ cup)
1 cup elbow macaroni or broken spaghetti
2 zucchini, sliced (about 2 cups)

Prepare Mini Meatballs. Mix tomatoes, beans, corn, water, wine, Italian seasoning, salt, pepper, celery and onion in 4-quart Dutch oven; break up tomatoes. Heat to boiling; add frozen Mini Meatballs. Cover and refrigerate no longer than 24 hours.

Heat meatball mixture to boiling. Add spaghetti and zucchini. Heat to boiling; reduce heat. Cover and simmer, stirring occasionally, until meatballs are hot and macaroni and zucchini are tender, about 12 minutes. Serve with grated Parmesan cheese if desired.

Mini Meatballs

1 pound ground beef
¼ cup dry bread crumbs
¼ cup milk
2 tablespoons chopped parsley
1 teaspoon fennel seed
½ teaspoon dried basil leaves
½ teaspoon salt
⅛ teaspoon pepper
1 small onion, chopped (about ¼ cup)
1 egg

Mix all ingredients. Shape mixture into about thirty-six 1-inch balls. (For ease in shaping meatballs, occasionally wet hands with cold water.) Place meatballs in lightly greased jelly roll pan, 15½×10½×1 inch, or 2 rectangular pans, 13×9×2 inches. Bake uncovered in 400° oven until brown, 15 to 20 minutes; cool slightly. Place meatballs on ungreased cookie sheet. Freeze uncovered until firm, about 3 hours. Place in freezer containers; label and freeze no longer than 3 months.

PER SERVING: Calories 220; Protein 13 g; Carbohydrate 27 g; Fat 7 g; Cholesterol 40 mg; Sodium 550 mg

Hamburger Minestrone

Calorie conscious? Use extra-lean ground beef, and save 40 calories per serving. Or try ground turkey, and you'll reduce calories by 95 per serving!

1 pound ground beef
½ cup chopped onion (about 1 medium)
1 clove garlic, crushed
1¼ cups water
1 cup thin slices celery (about 2 medium stalks)
1 cup sliced zucchini (about 1 small)
1 cup shredded cabbage
½ cup uncooked elbow macaroni or broken spaghetti
2 teaspoons beef bouillon granules
1 teaspoon Italian seasoning
1 can (28 ounces) whole tomatoes, undrained
1 can (8 ounces) kidney beans, undrained
1 can (8 ounces) whole kernel corn, undrained

Cook ground beef, onion and garlic in 4-quart Dutch oven, stirring occasionally, until beef is brown; drain. Stir in remaining ingredients; break up tomatoes.

Heat to boiling; reduce heat. Cover and simmer about 15 minutes, stirring occasionally, until macaroni is tender. Serve with grated Parmesan cheese if desired.   **6 servings**

PER SERVING: Calories 250; Protein 25 g; Carbohydrate 27 g; Fat 5 g; Cholesterol 55 mg; Sodium 700 mg

Rosemary Lamb Ragout

Ragout *is a French word, which means "to restore the appetite." This wonderful lamb stew will certainly please all appetites, from light to hearty.*

    2 pounds lamb boneless shoulder
    2 tablespoons vegetable oil
    2½ cups water
    1 cup dry white wine or water
    3 tablespoons tomato paste
    3 teaspoons chicken bouillon granules
    1 tablespoon chopped fresh or 1 tea-
        spoon dried rosemary leaves, crushed
    1 teaspoon chopped fresh or ½ teaspoon
        dried thyme leaves
    ¼ teaspoon pepper
    2 cloves garlic, finely chopped
    8 small red potatoes, cut in half
    6 small onions, cut into fourths
    3 medium carrots, cut into 1½-inch
        pieces
    3 small turnips, cut into fourths
    1 package (10 ounces) frozen green peas
    ¼ cup cold water
    2 tablespoons all-purpose flour

Trim excess fat from lamb shoulder. Cut lamb into 1-inch cubes. Sauté lamb in oil in Dutch oven over medium-high heat about 20 minutes or until brown; drain. Add 2½ cups water, the wine, tomato paste, bouillon granules, rosemary, thyme, pepper and garlic. Heat to boiling; reduce heat. Cover and simmer about 45 minutes or until lamb is almost tender.

Stir in potatoes, onions, carrots and turnips. Cover and simmer about 20 minutes or until vegetables are almost tender. Stir in peas. Cover and simmer about 10 minutes longer or until vegetables are tender.

Shake ¼ cup water and the flour in tightly covered container. Gradually stir into ragout. Heat to boiling, stirring constantly. Boil and stir 1 minute.

PORK RAGOUT: Substitute 2 pounds pork boneless loin for the lamb and beef bouillon granules for the chicken bouillon granules. Increase first simmering time to about 1 hour.   **6 servings**

PER SERVING: Calories 555; Protein 37 g; Carbohydrates 42 g; Fat 16 g; Cholesterol 110 mg; Sodium 510 mg

Green Chile Stew

Substitute Anaheim chiles for the poblano chiles to moderate the heat of the dish. This is a very fragrant stew, rich with the flavor of lamb and the accents of lemon peel and juniper berries.

3 pounds lamb boneless shoulder
1 large onion, chopped (about 1 cup)
3 cloves garlic, finely chopped
¼ cup vegetable oil
2 cups chicken broth
1 teaspoon salt
1 teaspoon dried juniper berries, crushed
¾ teaspoon pepper
1 tablespoon all-purpose flour
¼ cup water
4 medium poblano chiles, roasted, peeled (right), seeded and cut into 2 × ¼-inch strips
2 tablespoons finely shredded lemon peel

Trim excess fat from lamb shoulder; cut lamb into 1-inch cubes. Cook and stir lamb, onion and garlic in oil in 4-quart Dutch oven over medium heat until lamb is no longer pink; drain.

Stir in broth, salt, juniper berries and pepper. Heat to boiling; reduce heat. Cover and simmer, stirring occasionally, until lamb is tender, about 1 hour.

Shake flour and water in tightly covered container; stir into lamb mixture. Heat to boiling, stirring constantly. Boil and stir 1 minute. Stir in chiles. Sprinkle each serving with lemon peel.   **4 servings**

TO ROAST CHILES: Set oven control to broil. Arrange whole chiles with their top surfaces about 5 inches from the heat. (Some people cut a small slit in the shoulder of each chile, to prevent it from bursting.) Broil, turning occasionally, until the skin is blistered and evenly browned (*not* burned). Remove chiles to a plastic bag and close tightly; let chiles sit for 20 minutes, then peel.

PER SERVING: Calories 860; Protein 100 g; Carbohydrate 11 g; Fat 46 g; Cholesterol 315 mg; Sodium 1170 mg

Green Chile Stew

Pork Stew with Corn Bread Topping

1 small red bell pepper
1 small yellow bell pepper
1 pound pork boneless loin, cut into 1-inch cubes
½ pound bulk chorizo sausage
1 large onion, chopped (about 1 cup)
2 cloves garlic, finely chopped
1 cup beef broth
1 tablespoon dried basil leaves
1 tablespoon dried cilantro leaves
2 teaspoons ground red chiles
1 cup whole kernel corn
1 medium tomato, chopped (about 1 cup)
1 small butternut or acorn squash, pared and cut into ½-inch cubes (about 1 cup)
1 can (2¼ ounces) sliced ripe olives, drained (about ½ cup)
Corn Bread Topping (right)
Fresh Tomato Salsa (right)

Cut 5 thin slices from each bell pepper; reserve slices. Chop remaining bell peppers (about ½ cup each). Cook pork, sausage, onion and garlic in 4-quart Dutch oven over medium heat, stirring occasionally, until pork is no longer pink; drain. Stir in chopped bell peppers, broth, basil, cilantro and ground red chiles. Heat to boiling; reduce heat. Cover and simmer 30 minutes, stirring occasionally. Stir corn, tomato, squash and olives into meat mixture; cook 15 minutes longer.

Heat oven to 425°. Prepare Corn Bread Topping. Pour meat mixture into ungreased rectangular baking dish, 13×9×2 inches, or 3-quart shallow casserole. Pour Corn Bread Topping over meat mixture; carefully spread to cover, sealing to edge of dish. Arrange reserved bell pepper slices on top. Bake until topping is golden brown, 15 to 20 minutes. Serve with Fresh Tomato Salsa.   **8 servings**

Corn Bread Topping

1½ cups yellow cornmeal
½ cup all-purpose flour
1 cup sour cream
⅔ cup milk
¼ cup vegetable oil
2 teaspoons baking powder
½ teaspoon baking soda
½ teaspoon salt
1 egg

Mix all ingredients; beat vigorously 30 seconds.

Fresh Tomato Salsa

½ cup sliced green onions (with tops)
½ cup chopped green bell pepper
2 to 3 tablespoons lime juice
2 tablespoons chopped fresh cilantro
1 tablespoon finely chopped jalapeño chile
1 teaspoon finely chopped garlic (about 3 cloves)
½ teaspoon salt
3 medium tomatoes, seeded and chopped (about 3 cups)

Mix all ingredients.

PER SERVING: Calories 550; Protein 31 g; Carbohydrate 42 g; Fat 29 g; Cholesterol 125 mg; Sodium 1020 mg

Pork Stew with Corn Bread Topping

Pork Stew with Beer

Pungent fresh cilantro, serrano chiles and fragrant spices make this beer-spiked stew from Ecuador intriguing. Accompany this dish with soothing, hot cooked rice.

2 pounds pork boneless shoulder
1 tablespoon olive or vegetable oil
1 medium onion, chopped
2 cloves garlic, finely chopped
1 can (8¼ ounces) whole tomatoes, drained
1 red serrano chile, finely chopped
2 tablespoons chopped fresh cilantro
1 teaspoon salt
1 teaspoon ground cumin
½ teaspoon dried oregano leaves
1 can or bottle (12 ounces) beer
1 large red pepper, cut into 1-inch pieces
Hot cooked rice

Trim fat from pork; cut pork into 1-inch cubes. Heat oil in Dutch oven until hot. Cook pork over medium heat, stirring frequently, until all liquid is evaporated and pork is brown, about 25 minutes; remove with slotted spoon. Drain all but 2 tablespoons of fat from Dutch oven.

Cook and stir onion and garlic in Dutch oven over medium heat until onion is softened. Add tomatoes, chile, cilantro, salt, cumin and oregano; break up tomatoes. Heat to boiling; reduce heat. Simmer uncovered 10 minutes. Stir in pork and beer. Heat to boiling; reduce heat. Cover and simmer 45 minutes. Stir in red pepper. Heat to boiling; reduce heat. Simmer uncovered until pork is tender and sauce is thickened, about 15 minutes; skim off fat. Serve with rice.

4 servings

PER SERVING: Calories 670; Protein 56 g; Carbohydrate 41 g; Fat 31 g; Cholesterol 170 mg; Sodium 1170 mg

Posole

In Mexico, posole *is traditionally made on New Year's Day. This stew is thick with hominy, beans and pork.*

¼ cup vegetable oil
1 clove garlic, finely chopped
½ pound pork boneless shoulder, cut into ½-inch cubes
¼ cup all-purpose flour
1 medium onion, chopped (about ½ cup)
1 can (15 ounces) pinto beans, drained
1 can (30 ounces) hominy, drained
¼ cup chopped carrot
¼ cup chopped celery
¼ cup chopped green chiles
1 tablespoon ground red chiles
3 cups chicken broth
1 teaspoon salt
¼ teaspoon pepper
1½ teaspoons dried oregano leaves
1 small onion, chopped (about ¼ cup)
¼ cup chopped fresh cilantro
Lime wedges
Tortilla chips

Heat oil and garlic in 3-quart saucepan until oil is hot. Coat pork with flour. Cook and stir pork in oil over medium heat until brown; remove pork with slotted spoon and drain.

Cook and stir ½ cup onion in same saucepan until softened. Stir in beans, hominy, carrot, celery, green chiles, ground red chiles and broth. Heat to boiling; reduce heat. Cover and simmer 10 minutes.

Stir pork, salt and pepper into vegetable mixture. Heat to boiling; reduce heat. Cover and simmer 30 minutes. Sprinkle with oregano, ¼ cup onion and the cilantro. Serve with lime wedges and tortilla chips.

6 servings

PER SERVING: Calories 580; Protein 20 g; Carbohydrate 56 g; Fat 31 g; Cholesterol 30 mg; Sodium 1340 mg

Hot-and-Sour Soup

¼ pound pork boneless loin
½ teaspoon cornstarch
½ teaspoon salt
½ teaspoon soy sauce
6 medium dried black mushrooms
4-ounce block firm tofu
4 cups chicken broth
3 tablespoons white vinegar
1 tablespoon soy sauce
1 teaspoon salt
½ cup shredded canned bamboo shoots
2 tablespoons cornstarch
2 tablespoons cold water
¼ teaspoon white pepper
2 eggs, slightly beaten
2 tablespoons chopped green onion (with tops)
2 teaspoons red pepper sauce
½ teaspoon sesame oil

Trim fat from pork loin; cut pork with grain into 2-inch strips. Cut strips across grain into ⅛-inch slices. Stack slices; cut into thin strips. Toss pork, ½ teaspoon cornstarch, ½ teaspoon salt and ½ teaspoon soy sauce in medium bowl. Cover and refrigerate 15 minutes.

Soak mushrooms in hot water 20 minutes or until soft; drain. Rinse in warm water; drain. Squeeze out excess moisture. Remove and discard stems; cut caps into thin slices. Cut tofu into 1½ × ¼-inch pieces.

Heat broth, vinegar, 1 tablespoon soy sauce and 1 teaspoon salt to boiling in 3-quart saucepan. Stir in bamboo shoots, mushrooms, pork and tofu. Heat to boiling; reduce heat. Cover and simmer 5 minutes.

Mix 2 tablespoons cornstarch, the water and white pepper; stir into soup. Heat to rolling boil over high heat, stirring constantly. (If broth is not heated to a rolling boil, egg will not form threads.) Pour egg slowly into soup, stirring constantly with fork until egg forms threads. Stir in green onions, pepper sauce and sesame oil.   **5 servings**

PER SERVING: Calories 110; Protein 9 g; Carbohydrate 7 g; Fat 5 g; Cholesterol 85 mg; Sodium 1580 mg

Pork and Spaetzle Soup

1 pound ground pork
1 egg
½ cup dry bread crumbs
½ teaspoon ground sage
¼ teaspoon salt
¼ teaspoon pepper
1 tablespoon vegetable oil
2 cans (14½ ounces each) beef broth
¾ cup apple cider or apple juice
½ teaspoon ground sage
1 large unpared all-purpose apple, chopped
Spaetzle (right)
¼ cup chopped fresh parsley

Mix ground pork, egg, bread crumbs, ½ teaspoon sage, the salt and pepper. Shape mixture into 1-inch balls. Heat oil in Dutch oven until hot. Cook meatballs in hot oil over medium heat about 10 minutes, turning frequently, until brown.

Add beef broth, apple cider, ½ teaspoon sage and the apple. Heat to boiling; reduce heat. Cover and simmer 10 minutes. Heat to boiling. Prepare Spaetzle batter. Press Spaetzle batter through colander (preferably one with large holes), a few tablespoons at a time, into soup. Stir once or twice to prevent sticking. Cook about 5 minutes or until Spaetzle rise to surface and are tender. Stir in parsley. Heat until hot. **6 servings**

PER SERVING: Calories 350; Protein 23 g; Carbohydrate 30 g; Fat 15 g; Cholesterol 190 mg; Sodium 730 mg

Spaetzle

2 eggs, beaten
¼ cup milk or water
1 cup all-purpose flour*
¼ teaspoon salt
Dash of pepper

Mix all ingredients (batter will be thick).

*Do not use self-rising flour in this recipe.

Meatballs with Celery Cabbage Soup

6 ounces celery cabbage
6 ounces lean ground pork
1 egg white
1 tablespoon cornstarch
2 teaspoons sweet white wine or chicken broth
1 teaspoon light soy sauce
⅛ teaspoon white pepper
4 cups chicken broth or pork broth
1 teaspoon salt

Cut celery cabbage into ¾-inch pieces. Mix pork, egg white, cornstarch, wine, soy sauce, and white pepper; shape into ten 1-inch balls.

Heat broth and salt to boiling in 3-quart saucepan. Add celery cabbage; boil uncovered 2 minutes. Add meatballs; heat to boiling. Reduce heat, cover and simmer 2 minutes or until meatballs are done. **4 or 5 servings**

PER SERVING: Calories 160; Protein 14 g; Carbohydrate 4 g; Fat 10 g; Cholesterol 25 mg; Sodium 1390 mg

Meatballs with Celery Cabbage Soup

Pork Dumpling Soup

Siu mai skins are thinner than wontons and are round instead of square. If you can't find them, you can cut circles out of wonton skins and use them as a substitute. Pleat one side and fold over into a decorative half-moon shape.

½ **medium head green cabbage (about ½ pound)**
¼ **teaspoon salt**
½ **pound lean ground pork**
½ **teaspoon salt**
½ **egg white**
1 **teaspoon cornstarch**
Dash of white pepper
½ **teaspoon sugar**
1 **teaspoon dry white wine, if desired**
1 **green onion (with top), finely chopped**
24 **siu mai skins* (about ¾ pound)**
7 **cups chicken broth**
½ **teaspoon sesame oil**
1 **green onion (with top), finely chopped**

Place cabbage in food processor. Cover and finely chop. Sprinkle ¼ teaspoon salt over cab-

*Wonton skins can be substituted for siu mai skins. Cut off corners to make a circle.

bage in medium bowl. Let stand at room temperature 30 minutes. Squeeze excess water from cabbage. Mix cabbage, ground pork, ½ teaspoon salt, the egg white, cornstarch, white pepper, sugar, wine and 1 chopped green onion.

Hold siu mai skin in hand. (Cover remaining skins with plastic wrap to keep them pliable.) Wet the edge of half of the circle closest to fingers. Pinch 2 or 3 pleats into the wet edge. Place 1 heaping teaspoon pork mixture in center of skin. Fold circle in half, pressing pleated edge to unpleated edge to seal dumpling
Repeat with remaining skins.
(Cover filled dumplings with plastic wrap to keep them from drying out.)

Heat broth and ½ teaspoon sesame oil to boiling in Dutch oven; reduce heat. Heat 4 cups water to boiling in 3-quart saucepan; add 12 dumplings. Heat to boiling. Remove dumplings with slotted spoon; place in hot broth. Repeat with remaining dumplings.

For each serving, place 1 drop sesame oil in soup bowl. Add 4 dumplings and broth; sprinkle with chopped green onion. **6 servings**

PER SERVING: Calories 345; Protein 18 g; Carbohydrate 37 g; Fat 14 g; Cholesterol 30 mg; Sodium 1410 mg

Cheesy Ham and Leek Soup

2 tablespoons margarine or butter
1 cup sliced leeks
1 clove garlic, crushed
2 tablespoons all-purpose flour
⅛ teaspoon pepper
1 cup half-and-half
1 can (14½ ounces) chicken broth
1½ cups chopped fully cooked smoked
    ham (about 8 ounces)
1 cup shredded Jarlsberg or Swiss
    cheese (4 ounces)
½ cup pine nuts, toasted
1 tablespoon chopped fresh chives

Heat margarine in 2-quart saucepan over medium heat. Cook leeks and garlic in margarine about 2 minutes. Stir in flour and pepper. Stir in half-and-half and chicken broth. Heat to boiling, stirring constantly. Boil and stir 1 minute. Stir in ham, cheese and pine nuts until cheese is melted and soup is hot. Sprinkle with chives. **4 servings**

MICROWAVE DIRECTIONS: Place margarine, leeks and garlic in 2-quart microwavable casserole. Cover tightly and microwave on high 3 to 4 minutes, stirring after 2 minutes, until leeks are tender. Stir in flour and pepper. Stir in half-and-half and chicken broth. Cover tightly and microwave 7 to 9 minutes, stirring after 2 minutes, until mixture is slightly thickened. Stir in ham, cheese and pine nuts. Cover tightly and microwave 2 minutes. Sprinkle with chives.

PER SERVING: Calories 415; Protein 27 g; Carbohydrate 12 g; Fat 29 g; Cholesterol 75 mg; Sodium 1430 mg

Buying and Cleaning Leeks

Leeks should have crisp, firm stalks with white bulbs and bright green tops.

Leeks must be cleaned thoroughly. Trim both ends; remove green tops to within 2 inches of white part.

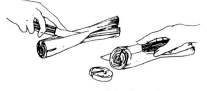

Peel outside layer of bulbs, then cut tops lengthwise but not through. Wash several times in water; drain.

Southwest Black Bean Soup

1 large onion, chopped (about 1 cup)
4 cloves garlic, finely chopped
2 tablespoons vegetable oil
1 pound dried black beans
6 cups chicken broth
2 cups cubed fully cooked smoked ham
2 tablespoons ground red chiles
2 tablespoons chopped fresh cilantro
1 tablespoon dried oregano leaves
2 teaspoons ground cumin
1 can (28 ounces) whole tomatoes,
  undrained
1 canned chipotle chile in adobo sauce
Quick Crème Fraîche (right)
Chopped red bell pepper

Cook and stir onion and garlic in oil in 4-quart Dutch oven over medium heat until onion is softened. Stir in remaining ingredients except Quick Crème Fraîche and bell pepper; heat to boiling. Boil 2 minutes; reduce heat. Cover and simmer until beans are tender, about 2 hours 15 minutes.

Pour one-quarter of the soup in blender or food processor. Cover and blend or process until smooth. Repeat with remaining soup. Serve with Quick Crème Fraîche and bell pepper.

8 servings

PER SERVING: Calories 440; Protein 25 g; Carbohydrate 45 g; Fat 18 g; Cholesterol 45 mg; Sodium 1150 mg

Quick Crème Fraîche

⅓ cup whipping (heavy) cream
⅔ cup sour cream

Gradually stir whipping cream into sour cream. Cover and refrigerate up to 48 hours.

Southwest Black Bean Soup

Senate Bean Soup

This is served every day in the cafeteria of the U.S. Senate—hence its name.

2 cups dried navy beans (about 1 pound)
12 cups water
1 ham bone
2½ cups mashed cooked potatoes
2 teaspoons salt
¼ teaspoon pepper
2 stalks celery, chopped (about 1 cup)
1 large onion, chopped (about 1 cup)
1 clove garlic, finely chopped

Heat beans and water to boiling in Dutch oven. Boil uncovered 2 minutes; remove from heat. Cover and let stand 1 hour.

Add ham bone. Heat to boiling; reduce heat. Cover and simmer about 2 hours or until beans are tender. Stir in remaining ingredients. Cover and simmer 1 hour. Remove ham bone. Remove ham from bone and cut into bite-size pieces. Stir into soup.   **12 servings**

PER SERVING: Calories 95; Protein 6 g; Carbohydrate 16 g; Fat 1 g; Cholesterol 8 mg; Sodium 660 mg

Easy Cassoulet

This dish thickens as it stands, and you can thin it with a little wine if you wish. It's an excellent company dish, using kitchen staples, and can be made quickly on short notice.

1 pound Polish or smoked sausage, diagonally sliced into 1-inch pieces
½ cup dry red wine or beef broth
2 tablespoons packed brown sugar
2 tablespoons chopped fresh or 1½ teaspoons dried thyme leaves
3 medium carrots, thinly sliced
2 small onions, thinly sliced and separated into rings
2 cloves garlic, finely chopped
1 can (15½ ounces) great northern beans, drained
1 can (15 ounces) kidney beans, drained
1 can (15 ounces) black beans, drained
1 can (15 ounces) tomato sauce

Heat oven to 375°. Mix all ingredients in ungreased 3-quart casserole. Cover and bake 50 to 60 minutes or until hot and bubbly and carrots are tender.   **8 servings**

MICROWAVE DIRECTIONS: Place carrots and wine in 3-quart microwavable casserole. Cover and microwave on high 5 minutes. Place sausage on carrots. Mix remaining ingredients. Pour over top. Cover tightly and microwave 18 to 22 minutes, stirring after 12 minutes, until hot and bubbly.

PER SERVING: Calories 260; Protein 18 g; Carbohydrate 35 g; Fat 5 g; Cholesterol 30 mg; Sodium 1260 mg

Couscous Soup with Sausage

1 tablespoon chopped jalapeño chiles
1 tablespoon olive or vegetable oil
½ teaspoon ground cumin
2 cloves garlic, crushed
1 pound fully cooked smoked sausage, cut crosswise into ¼-inch slices
2½ cups water
1 can (10¾ ounces) condensed chicken broth
½ cup couscous
2 tablespoons chopped fresh or 2 teaspoons dried mint leaves
¼ teaspoon pepper
1 medium tomato, seeded and chopped

Cook chiles, oil, cumin, garlic and sausage in 3-quart saucepan over medium heat about 8 minutes or until sausage is brown; drain.

Add water and chicken broth. Heat to boiling. Stir in couscous, mint and pepper; reduce heat. Cover and simmer 5 minutes. Stir in tomato. Serve with chopped parsley, finely chopped garlic and lemon juice if desired. **4 servings**

MICROWAVE DIRECTIONS: Omit oil. Place chiles, cumin, garlic and sausage in 3-quart microwavable casserole. Cover tightly and microwave on high 2 minutes. Add water and chicken broth. Cover tightly and microwave 5 minutes. Stir in couscous, mint and pepper. Cover tightly and microwave 3 minutes. Stir in tomato. Let stand covered 5 minutes. Continue as directed.

PER SERVING: Calories 405; Protein 20 g; Carbohydrate 5 g; Fat 34 g; Cholesterol 70 mg; Sodium 1115 mg

Southwest Chicken Soup (page 35)

2

Pleasing Poultry

Chicken and Broth

3- to 3½-pound cut-up broiler-fryer chicken*
4½ cups cold water
1 teaspoon salt
½ teaspoon pepper
1 stalk celery with leaves, cut up
1 medium carrot, cut up
1 small onion, cut up
1 sprig parsley

Remove any excess fat from chicken. Place chicken, giblets (except liver) and neck in Dutch oven. Add remaining ingredients and heat to boiling. Skim foam from broth; reduce heat. Cover and simmer about 45 minutes or until juices of chicken run clear.

*3 to 3½ pounds chicken necks, backs and giblets (except liver) can be used to make broth.

Remove chicken from broth. Cool chicken about 10 minutes or just until cool enough to handle. Strain broth through cheesecloth-lined sieve; discard vegetables. Remove skin and bones from chicken. Cut up chicken. Skim fat from broth. Cover and refrigerate broth and chicken in separate containers no longer than 24 hours, or freeze for future use. **About 3 cups cooked chicken; about 3 cups broth**

PER CUP: Calories 335; Protein 38 g; Carbohydrate 0 g; Fat 19 g; Cholesterol 125 mg; Sodium 115 mg

Chicken-Noodle Soup

A marvelously soothing soup that is welcome when you have a cold or the flu or just about any time.

Chicken and Broth (page 00)
2 medium carrots, sliced (about 1 cup)
2 medium stalks celery, sliced (about 1 cup)
1 small onion, chopped (about ¼ cup)
1 tablespoon chicken bouillon granules
1 cup uncooked medium noodles (about 2 ounces)

Prepare Chicken and Broth. Reserve cut-up chicken. Add enough water to broth to measure 5 cups. Heat broth, carrots, celery, onion and bouillon granules to boiling; reduce heat. Cover and simmer about 15 minutes or until carrots are tender. Stir in noodles and chicken. Heat to boiling; reduce heat. Simmer uncovered 7 to 10 minutes or until noodles are tender. Sprinkle with chopped parsley if desired.

6 servings

CHICKEN-RICE SOUP: Substitute ½ cup uncooked regular long grain rice for the uncooked noodles. Stir in rice with the vegetables. Cover and simmer about 15 minutes or until rice is tender. Stir in chicken and heat until chicken is hot.

PER SERVING: Calories 295; Protein 31 g; Carbohydrate 7 g; Fat 15 g; Cholesterol 90m g; Sodium 670 mg

Chicken-Cabbage Soup

If you are concerned about sodium and would like to lower your sodium consumption, use low-sodium eight-vegetable juice and bouillon granules.

5 cups finely chopped cabbage (about 1¼ pounds)
3 cups eight-vegetable juice
2 cups water
2 cups ¼-inch slices carrots (about 4 medium)
1 cup chopped celery (about 2 medium stalks)
1 medium onion, sliced
2 tablespoons chicken bouillon granules
¼ teaspoon pepper
3 to 3½ pounds broiler-fryer chicken pieces
½ teaspoon paprika
2 tablespoons reduced-calorie margarine

Heat cabbage, vegetable juice, water, carrots, celery, onion, bouillon granules and pepper to boiling in 4-quart Dutch oven; reduce heat. Cover and simmer 30 minutes.

Remove skin and any excess fat from chicken pieces. Cut each breast half into halves. Sprinkle chicken with paprika. Heat margarine in 10-inch nonstick skillet. Cook chicken 15 to 20 minutes or until light brown on all sides. Add chicken to soup mixture. Heat to boiling; reduce heat. Cover and simmer about 30 minutes or until juices of thickest chicken pieces run clear. Serve chicken pieces in soup bowls; pour soup over chicken.

6 servings

PER SERVING: Calories 315; Protein 39 g; Carbohydrate 17 g; Fat 10 g; Cholesterol 110 mg; Sodium 850 mg

Chicken and Vegetable Stew

This flavorful Caribbean stew is spiced with hot chile and chock full of such tempting vegetables as sweet potatoes, sweet corn and winter squash. It is especially popular in the Dominican Republic.

2½- to 3-pound cut-up broiler-fryer
   chicken
6 cups water
2 tablespoons beef bouillon granules
¼ pound winter squash, pared and cut
   into ½-inch pieces (about 1 cup)
½ cup fresh or frozen green peas
2 teaspoons salt
¼ teaspoon pepper
1 small hot chile, stemmed, seeded and
   sliced
2 medium tomatoes, chopped
2 medium onions, chopped
2 medium potatoes, cut into ½-inch
   slices
2 medium sweet potatoes or yams, cut
   into ½-inch slices
3 ears sweet corn, cut into 3 pieces
Chopped fresh chives

Heat chicken, water and bouillon granules to boiling in Dutch oven; reduce heat. Cover and simmer 30 minutes. Skim off fat. Add remaining ingredients except chives. Heat to boiling; reduce heat. Cover and simmer about 20 minutes or until thickest pieces of chicken are done and vegetables are tender. Garnish each serving with chives.   **8 or 9 servings**

PER SERVING: Calories 270; Protein 21 g; Carbohydrate 29 g; Fat 8 g; Cholesterol 50 mg; Sodium 1560 mg

Mulligatawny Soup

Mulligatawny is an Indian spice-filled soup adapted to British tastes in the days of colonial strength. Cloves and mace add a deep note to this chicken-filled broth.

2½- to 3-pound cut-up broiler-fryer
   chicken
4 cups water
1½ teaspoons salt
1 teaspoon curry powder
1 teaspoon lemon juice
⅛ teaspoon ground cloves
⅛ teaspoon ground mace
1 medium onion, chopped
2 tablespoons margarine or butter
2 tablespoons all-purpose flour
1 medium carrot, thinly sliced
1 apple, chopped
1 medium green pepper, cut into ½-inch
   pieces
2 medium tomatoes, chopped
Parsley

Heat chicken, water, salt, curry powder, lemon juice, cloves and mace to boiling in Dutch oven; reduce heat. Cover and simmer until thickest pieces of chicken are done, about 45 minutes. Remove chicken and broth; skim fat from broth if necessary. Add enough water to broth if necessary to measure 4 cups. Remove bones and skin from chicken; cut chicken into pieces.

Cook and stir onion in margarine in Dutch oven over medium heat until softened. Remove from heat; stir in flour. Gradually stir in broth. Add chicken, carrot, apple, green pepper and tomatoes. Heat to boiling; reduce heat. Cover and simmer until carrot is tender, about 10 minutes. Serve in shallow soup bowls; garnish with parsley.   **6 servings**

PER SERVING: Calories 200; Protein 20 g; Carbohydrate 12 g; Fat 8 g; Cholesterol 55 mg; Sodium 640 mg

Chicken and Corn Chowder

Although often prepared with fish or shellfish, a chowder is actually any rich soup, usually milk-based, that contains solid ingredients. This Pennsylvania Dutch recipe is thick with diced chicken, tender corn kernels and rivels, *diminutive dumplings that are added just a few minutes before the chowder is served.*

3- to 3½-pound cut-up broiler-fryer chicken
6 cups water
1 medium onion, sliced
3 medium stalks celery (with leaves), finely chopped (about 1½ cups)
1 medium carrot, chopped (about ½ cup)
2 teaspoons salt
1 can (17 ounces) cream-style corn
2 hard-cooked eggs, finely chopped
Egg Rivels (right)

Remove any excess fat from chicken. Place chicken, giblets (except liver) and neck in Dutch oven. Add water, onion, celery, carrot and salt; heat to boiling. Skim foam from broth; reduce heat. Cover and simmer about 1½ hours or until thickest pieces of chicken are done.

Remove chicken from broth; cool chicken about 10 minutes or just until cool enough to handle. Remove chicken from bones and skin; cut chicken into small pieces. Skim fat from broth; return chicken to broth. Stir in corn and eggs. Heat to boiling; reduce heat. Sprinkle with Egg Rivel mixture; stir into soup. Simmer uncovered 10 minutes. **8 servings**

Egg Rivels

1 cup all-purpose flour
¼ teaspoon salt
1 egg

Mix all ingredients until mixture looks like cornmeal.

PER SERVING: Calories 260; Protein 23 g; Carbohydrate 25 g; Fat 8 g; Cholesterol 130 mg; Sodium 840 mg

Chicken and Corn Chowder

Edible Bowls

Edible bowls are a fun way to serve up soup. Place edible bowls on dinner plates before filling.

Snazzy Bell Pepper Bowls

Cut thin slices from stem of peppers; remove seeds and membranes. Fill bell peppers just before serving; replace tops.

Sunny Squash Bowls

Cut round winter squash, such as acorn or buttercup, lengthwise in half; remove seeds and fibers. Cook squash as desired before filling.

Chewy Bread Bowls

Cut off tops of small, round bread loaves, and scoop out the bread from the loaves, leaving a 1-inch-thick wall. Fill loaves; replace tops.

Crispy Tortilla Bowls

Brush both sides of tortillas with melted margarine. Place each tortilla in ovenproof bowl, making pleats as needed to fit. Bake tortillas in bowls in 400° oven for 10 to 15 minutes or until crisp and golden brown. Cool tortillas in bowls.

Chicken and Dumplings

3- to 3½-pound cut-up stewing chicken
4 celery stalk tops
1 medium carrot, sliced
1 small onion, sliced
2 sprigs fresh parsley, snipped
1 teaspoon salt
⅛ teaspoon pepper
5 cups water
½ cup variety baking mix
2 cups variety baking mix
⅔ cup milk

Remove any excess fat from chicken. Place chicken, giblets (except liver), neck, celery, carrot, onion, parsley, salt, pepper and water in Dutch oven. Cover and heat to boiling; reduce heat. Cook over low heat about 2 hours or until chicken is done. Remove chicken and vegetables. Skim ½ cup fat from broth; reserve. Remove broth; reserve 4 cups. Heat reserved fat in Dutch oven; blend in ½ cup baking mix. Cook over low heat, stirring constantly, until mixture is smooth and bubbly; remove from heat. Stir in reserved broth. Heat to boiling, stirring constantly. Boil and stir 1 minute. Return chicken and vegetables to Dutch oven; heat through.

Mix 2 cups baking mix and the milk until soft dough forms. Drop by spoonfuls onto hot chicken mixture. Cook uncovered over low heat 10 minutes; cover and cook 10 minutes longer. **4 to 6 servings**

PER SERVING: Calories 655; Protein 47 g; Carbohydrate 52 g; Fat 29 g; Cholesterol 130 mg; Sodium 1170 mg

Chicken Gumbo

3- to 4-pound cut-up broiler-fryer chicken
2 cups water or chicken broth
1 cup chopped celery tops
2 teaspoons salt
1 medium onion, sliced
1 clove garlic, crushed
1 large bay leaf
1 medium onion, chopped (about ½ cup)
1 small green pepper, chopped (about ½ cup)
2 tablespoons margarine or butter
¼ cup snipped parsley
½ teaspoon red pepper sauce
1 can (28 ounces) whole tomatoes, undrained
1½ cups sliced fresh or frozen okra
⅓ cup uncooked long grain rice
Dash of pepper
1½ teaspoons filé powder

Remove any excess fat from chicken. Heat chicken, giblets (except liver), neck, water, celery tops, salt, sliced onion, garlic and bay leaf to boiling; reduce heat. Cover and simmer until thickest pieces of chicken are done, about 45 minutes.

Remove chicken from broth; cool chicken 10 minutes. Remove chicken from bones and skin; cut chicken into bite-size pieces. Skim fat from broth; strain broth. Place broth and chicken in Dutch oven.

Cook and stir chopped onion and green pepper in margarine over medium heat until onion is softened. Stir onion mixture, parsley, pepper sauce and tomatoes into chicken and broth; break up tomatoes. Heat to boiling; reduce heat. Simmer uncovered 15 minutes.

Stir in okra, rice and pepper. Heat to boiling; reduce heat. Cover and simmer until rice is done, about 15 minutes. Remove from heat; stir in filé powder. Remove bay leaf; serve. (Soup can be prepared ahead; stir in filé powder after reheating.)   **8 servings**

PER SERVING: Calories 210; Protein 20 g; Carbohydrate 17 g; Fat 7 g; Cholesterol 50 mg; Sodium 880 mg

Country Captain

Country Captain

Was this dish brought to the port of Savannah by the captain of a spice ship, as Georgians claim, or was it the invention of a local cook desperately tired of fried chicken? Whichever version they believed, cooks knew the exotic spices, blended to make curry powder today, would make a memorable dish when combined with plentiful regional foods.

½ cup all-purpose flour
1 teaspoon salt
¼ teaspoon pepper
2½- to 3-pound cut-up broiler-fryer chicken
¼ cup vegetable oil
1½ teaspoons curry powder
½ teaspoon dried thyme leaves
¼ teaspoon salt
1 large onion, chopped (about 1 cup)
1 green pepper, chopped (about 1½ cups)
1 clove garlic, finely chopped
1 can (16 ounces) whole tomatoes, undrained
¼ cup currants or raisins
⅓ cup slivered almonds, toasted
3 cups hot cooked rice

Heat oven to 350°. Mix flour, 1 teaspoon salt and the pepper. Coat chicken with flour mixture. Heat oil in 10-inch skillet until hot. Cook chicken over medium heat until light brown, 15 to 20 minutes. Place chicken in ungreased 2½-quart casserole. Drain oil from skillet.

Add curry powder, thyme, ¼ teaspoon salt, the onion, green pepper, garlic and tomatoes to skillet. Heat to boiling, stirring frequently to loosen brown particles from skillet. Pour over chicken. Cover and bake until thickest pieces are done, about 40 minutes. Skim fat from liquid if necessary; add currants. Bake uncovered 5 minutes. Sprinkle with almonds. Serve with rice and, if desired, grated fresh coconut and chutney.

6 servings

PER SERVING: Calories 530; Protein 29 g; Carbohydrate 50 g; Fat 24 g; Cholesterol 70 mg; Sodium 1020 mg

Brunswick Stew

Once prepared with squirrel and other small woodland animals, this stew evolved into a dish usually made with chicken or turkey and vegetables. Still popular in its native Brunswick County, Virginia, it is often cooked in great steaming kettles and served at outdoor gatherings.

3- to 3½-pound cut-up broiler-fryer chicken
2 cups water
1 teaspoon salt
¼ teaspoon pepper
Dash of ground red pepper
2 cans (16 ounces each) whole tomatoes, undrained
1 can (17 ounces) whole kernel corn, undrained
1 can (14 ounces) lima beans, undrained
1 medium potato, cut into cubes (about 1 cup)
1 medium onion, chopped (about ½ cup)
¼ pound lean salt pork, cut into 1-inch pieces
½ cup water
2 tablespoons all-purpose flour

Remove any excess fat from chicken. Heat chicken, giblets (except liver), neck, 2 cups water and salt to boiling in Dutch oven; reduce heat. Cover and simmer about 1 hour or until thickest pieces of chicken are done.

Remove chicken from broth; cool chicken about 10 minutes or just until cool enough to handle. Skim fat from broth. Remove skin and bones from chicken if desired; return chicken to broth. Stir in pepper, red pepper, tomatoes, corn, beans, potato, onion and salt pork. Heat to boiling; reduce

heat. Simmer uncovered 1 hour. Shake ½ cup water and the flour in tightly covered container. Stir into stew. Heat to boiling, stirring constantly. Boil and stir 1 minute.   **8 servings**

PER SERVING: Calories 290; Protein 23 g; Carbohydrate 23 g; Fat 12 g; Cholesterol 55 mg; Sodium 730 mg

Harvest Chicken Stew

4 cups 1-inch cubes peeled eggplant (about 1 pound)
4 cups ⅛-inch slices small red potatoes (about 8)
2 cups sliced carrots (about 4 medium)
3 medium onions, cut into fourths
⅔ cup chopped fresh parsley
3 cups chicken broth
2 tablespoons chopped fresh or 2 teaspoons dried thyme leaves
¼ teaspoon salt
¼ teaspoon pepper
½ cup cold water
2 tablespoons all-purpose flour
6 skinless boneless chicken breast halves (about 1½ pounds), cut into fourths
¼ cup tomato paste
2 tablespoons lemon juice

Heat oven to 350°. Mix eggplant, potatoes, carrots, onions, parsley, broth, thyme, salt and pepper in Dutch oven. Cover and bake 50 minutes. Shake cold water and flour in tightly covered container. Stir flour mixture, chicken, tomato paste and lemon juice into stew. Cover and bake about 20 minutes or until potatoes are tender and juices of chicken run clear.

6 servings

PER SERVING: Calories 375; Protein 34 g; Carbohydrate 49 g; Fat 5 g; Cholesterol 65 mg; Sodium 650 mg

Chicken-Tortellini Soup

¼ cup margarine or butter (½ stick)
½ cup finely chopped onion
½ cup finely chopped celery
4 skinless boneless chicken breast
    halves, cut into 1-inch pieces (about
    1½ pounds)
¼ cup all-purpose flour
½ teaspoon pepper
4½ cups chicken broth
1 package (16 ounces) cheese-filled tortel-
    lini, cooked
Parmesan cheese

Heat margarine in large saucepan until melted. Cook and stir onion, celery and chicken in margarine over medium heat about 8 minutes or until chicken is done. Stir in flour and pepper; gradually add chicken broth. Cook over medium heat, stirring constantly until mixture boils; boil 1 minute. Stir in tortellini; heat until warm. Serve with Parmesan cheese. **8 servings**

PER SERVING: Calories 300; Protein 23 g; Carbohydrate 18 g; Fat 15 g; Cholesterol 120 mg; Sodium 290 mg

Southwest Chicken Soup

You can substitute marinated or pickled red peppers for the fresh. They are available in many supermarkets in the refrigerated or shelf-stable sections. Be sure to drain the light brine in which they are packaged before using.

2 large red bell peppers
4 skinless boneless chicken breast
    halves (about 1 pound)
½ cup chopped onion (about 1 medium)
3 cups chicken broth
2 tablespoons lime juice
1 tablespoon chopped fresh cilantro
½ teaspoon salt
¼ teaspoon pepper
2 cloves garlic, crushed
2 cups cubed jicama

Set oven control to broil. Place bell peppers on rack in broiler pan. Broil with tops about 5 inches from heat, turning occasionally, until skin is blistered and evenly browned (not burned). Remove peppers to brown paper bag and close tightly. Let stand 20 minutes.

Place chicken breasts on rack in broiler pan. Broil with tops 5 to 7 inches from heat about 15 minutes, turning once, until juices of chicken run clear. Cool 10 minutes. Cut into bite-size pieces.

Pare peppers; discard skin. Place peppers and onion in blender or food processor. Cover and blend or process until smooth.

Heat pepper mixture, broth, lime juice, cilantro, salt, pepper and garlic to boiling in 2-quart saucepan; reduce heat. Simmer uncovered 15 minutes, stirring occasionally. Stir in chicken and jicama. Heat until hot. **4 servings**

PER SERVING: Calories 215; Protein 33 g; Carbohydrate 13 g; Fat 3 g; Cholesterol 70 mg; Sodium 980 mg

Wonton Soup

¼ pound raw medium shrimp (in shells)
2 ounces lean ground pork
3 whole water chestnuts, finely chopped
2 green onions (with tops), chopped
1 teaspoon cornstarch
½ teaspoon salt
¼ teaspoon sesame oil
Dash of white pepper
24 wonton skins
1 egg white, slightly beaten
5 cups water
½ chicken breast (about ½ pound)
½ teaspoon cornstarch
½ teaspoon salt
Dash of white pepper
4 ounces Chinese pea pods
4 ounces mushrooms
4 cups chicken broth
¼ cup sliced canned bamboo shoots
1 teaspoon salt
Dash of white pepper
2 tablespoons chopped green onions
   (with tops)
¼ teaspoon sesame oil

Peel shrimp. Make a shallow cut lengthwise down back of each shrimp; wash out vein. Chop shrimp finely. Mix shrimp, pork, water chestnuts, 2 green onions, 1 teaspoon cornstarch, ½ teaspoon salt, ¼ teaspoon sesame oil and dash of white pepper.

Place ½ teaspoon shrimp mixture in center of wonton skin. (Cover remaining skins with plastic wrap to keep them pliable.) Fold bottom corner of wonton skin over filling to opposite corner, forming a triangle. Brush right corner of triangle with egg white. Bring corners together below filling; pinch left corner to right corner to seal. Repeat with remaining wonton skins. (Cover filled wontons with plastic wrap to keep them from drying out.)

Heat water to boiling in Dutch oven; add wontons. Heat to boiling; reduce heat. Simmer uncovered 2 minutes; drain. Rinse wontons under cold water; place in bowl and cover with iced water to keep them from sticking together.

Remove bones and skin from chicken breast; cut chicken into thin slices. Toss chicken, ½ teaspoon cornstarch, ½ teaspoon salt and dash of white pepper in medium bowl. Cover and refrigerate 20 minutes. Remove strings from pea pods. Place pea pods in boiling water. Cover and cook 1 minute; drain. Immediately rinse in cold water; drain. Cut pea pods lengthwise into halves. Cut mushrooms into ¼-inch slices.

Heat broth and mushrooms to boiling in Dutch oven. Stir in chicken; heat to boiling. Drain wontons. Stir wontons, bamboo shoots, 1 teaspoon salt and dash of white pepper into broth. Heat to boiling; reduce heat. Simmer uncovered 2 minutes. Stir in pea pods, 2 tablespoons green onions and ¼ teaspoon sesame oil.

8 servings

PER SERVING: Calories 265; Protein 15 g; Carbohydrate 35 g; Fat 7 g; Cholesterol 35 mg; Sodium 1170 mg

Dumpling Soup

The dumplings in this soup are called gnocchi in Italy, and are made from a satisfying mixture of potatoes, eggs and flour.

2 tablespoons olive oil
2 cloves garlic, finely chopped
1 medium onion, thinly sliced
1 pound chicken livers, cut up
4 cups chicken broth
2 cups water
½ cup dry white wine, if desired
½ cup chopped fresh parsley
½ teaspoon pepper
1 bay leaf
1 medium potato, boiled, peeled and mashed (about ⅔ cup)
1 cup all-purpose flour
1 jumbo egg

Heat oil in 4-quart Dutch oven over medium-high heat. Sauté garlic and onion in oil. Stir in chicken livers; cook over medium heat about 5 minutes, stirring frequently, until livers are brown. Stir in chicken broth, water, wine, parsley, pepper and bay leaf. Heat to boiling; reduce heat. Simmer uncovered 40 minutes.

Mix potato, flour and egg. Shape mixture into 1-inch balls. (Coat hands with flour, if necessary, to prevent sticking.) Remove bay leaf from soup. Heat soup to boiling; add the dumplings. When dumplings rise to the surface, boil 4 minutes longer.   **6 servings**

PER SERVING: Calories 255; Protein 19 g; Carbohydrate 24 g; Fat 9 g; Cholesterol 340 mg; Sodium 360 mg

Handling Raw Poultry

Raw chicken should be handled properly to ensure food safety. These tips will help you when cooking with raw chicken.

• When cutting up raw poultry and meat, choose a plastic cutting surface rather than a wooden board. You'll find the plastic one less porous and easier to clean.
• After handling raw chicken, wash your hands carefully before touching other foods that are not going to be cooked— salad fixings, for example.
• Be sure to thoroughly clean the cutting surface, counter top and all utensils used in the preparation of the chicken. Wooden cutting boards can be washed with a solution of 1 teaspoon chlorine bleach and ½ teaspoon vinegar to 2 quarts water.

Chicken Tortilla Soup

Based on the traditional Mexican soup sopa azteca, this rich broth features crisp fried tortilla strips and creamy slices of avocado.

1 medium onion, finely chopped (about ½ cup)
1 clove garlic, finely chopped
2 tablespoons vegetable oil
4 cups chicken broth
¼ cup chopped red bell pepper
1 teaspoon ground red chiles
¾ teaspoon dried basil leaves
½ teaspoon salt
¼ teaspoon pepper
1 can (15 ounces) tomato purée
½ cup vegetable oil
10 corn tortillas (6 inches in diameter), cut into ½-inch strips
2 cups cut-up cooked chicken breasts
Shredded Monterey Jack or Chihuahua cheese
Avocado slices

Cook and stir onion and garlic in 2 tablespoons oil in 4-quart Dutch oven over medium heat until onion is softened. Stir in broth, bell pepper, ground red chiles, basil, salt, pepper and tomato purée. Heat to boiling; reduce heat. Simmer uncovered 30 minutes.

Heat ½ cup oil in 10-inch skillet until hot. Cook tortilla strips in oil until light golden brown, 30 to 60 seconds; drain. Divide tortilla strips and chicken among 6 bowls; pour broth over chicken. Top with cheese and avocado slices.

6 servings

PER SERVING: Calories 450; Protein 29 g; Carbohydrate 29 g; Fat 24 g; Cholesterol 65 mg; Sodium 1260 mg

Chicken and Leek Soup

1 package (1.8 ounces) leek soup and recipe mix (dry)
½ cup uncooked quick barley
1 cup milk
1½ cups cut-up cooked chicken

Prepare soup as directed on package—except add barley and increase milk to 1 cup. Stir chicken in with the milk. **4 servings**

PER SERVING: Calories 210; Protein 21 g; Carbohydrate 23 g; Fat 4 g; Cholesterol 45 mg; Sodium 110 mg

Chicken and Leek Soup

Oriental-style Chicken-Noodle Soup

3 cups water
1 package (3 ounces) chicken flavor Oriental-style 3-minute noodles
2 cups cut-up cooked chicken
2 medium stalks bok choy (with leaves), cut into ¼-inch slices
1 medium carrot, sliced
1 teaspoon sesame oil, if desired

Heat water to boiling in 3-quart saucepan. Break apart block of noodles into water; stir in chicken, bok choy and carrot.

Heat to boiling; reduce heat. Simmer uncovered 3 minutes, stirring occasionally. Stir in Flavor Packet and sesame oil. **4 servings**

PER SERVING: Calories 130; Protein 22 g; Carbohydrate 4 g; Fat 3 g; Cholesterol 55 mg; Sodium 160 mg

Chicken and Broccoli Chowder

2 cups water
⅓ cup chopped onion
2 teaspoons chicken bouillon granules
1 package (10 ounces) frozen chopped broccoli
1⅓ cups mashed potato mix (dry)
2 cups cut-up cooked chicken
2 cups shredded Swiss cheese (8 ounces)
2 cups milk
½ teaspoon salt

Heat water, onion, bouillon granules and broccoli to boiling in 3-quart saucepan; reduce heat. Cover and simmer 5 minutes.

Stir in potato mix until well blended; stir in remaining ingredients. Heat over low heat, stirring occasionally, until hot and cheese is melted, about 5 minutes. **6 servings**

PER SERVING: Calories 320; Protein 30 g; Carbohydrate 18 g; Fat 14 g; Cholesterol 75 mg; Sodium 790 mg

Turkey and Wild Rice Soup

3½ cups water
½ cup uncooked wild rice
½ cup chopped onion (about 1 medium)
1 tablespoon chicken bouillon granules
2 turkey drumsticks (about 1½ pounds)
2 medium stalks celery with leaves, sliced
2 bay leaves
1 can (16 ounces) stewed tomatoes

Mix all ingredients in Dutch oven. Heat to boiling; reduce heat. Cover and simmer 50 to 60 minutes or until turkey is done and wild rice is tender.

Remove turkey drumsticks; cool about 5 minutes. Remove skin and bones. Cut turkey into bite-size pieces. Stir turkey into soup. Heat until hot. Remove bay leaves. **6 servings**

PER SERVING: Calories 260; Protein 34 g; Carbohydrate 16 g; Fat 7 g; Cholesterol 105 mg; Sodium 510 mg

Oriental Broth with Turkey

1 pound ground turkey
1 egg
½ cup dry bread crumbs
1½ teaspoons finely chopped gingerroot
  or ½ teaspoon ground ginger
¼ teaspoon salt
¼ teaspoon pepper
1 teaspoon sesame or vegetable oil
2 large stalks bok choy with leaves
2 cups thinly sliced carrots (about 4
  medium)
1 cup dry white wine or chicken broth
2 cans (14½ ounces each) chicken broth

Mix ground turkey, egg, bread crumbs, gingerroot, salt and pepper. Shape into 1-inch balls. Cook in oil in nonstick Dutch oven over medium heat about 10 minutes, turning frequently, until brown.

Separate bok choy leaves from stalks. Cut leaves into thin strips; reserve. Cut stalks into ¼-inch slices. Stir bok choy stalks, carrots, wine and broth into Dutch oven. Heat to boiling; reduce heat. Cover and simmer about 20 minutes or until vegetables are crisp-tender. Stir in bok choy leaves just until wilted.   **6 servings**

PER SERVING: Calories 235; Protein 22 g; Carbohydrate 10 g; Fat 8 g; Cholesterol 85 mg; Sodium 660 mg

Turkey Tortellini Soup

1 package (7 ounces) dried cheese-filled
  tortellini
2¼ cups water
2 tablespoons rice wine vinegar or white
  wine vinegar
2 tablespoons soy sauce
1 can (10¾ ounces) condensed chicken
  broth
1 to 2 tablespoons finely chopped gingerroot or 1 to 2 teaspoons ground
  ginger
3 large stalks bok choy with leaves
2 cups cut-up cooked turkey (about 10
  ounces)
¼ cup sliced green onions with tops
  (about 2 medium)
1 cup enoki mushrooms

Cook tortellini as directed on package; drain. Heat water, vinegar, soy sauce, broth and gingerroot to boiling in 3-quart saucepan; reduce heat.

Separate bok choy leaves from stalks. Cut leaves into thin strips; reserve. Cut stalks into ¼-inch slices. Stir bok choy stalks, turkey and onions into broth mixture. Simmer uncovered 15 minutes. Stir in bok choy leaves and mushrooms. Simmer just until leaves are wilted.

4 servings

PER SERVING: Calories 350; Protein 30 g; Carbohydrate 41 g; Fat 7 g; Cholesterol 60 mg; Sodium 1070 mg

Baja Seafood Stew (page 57)

3

Satisfying Seafood

Fish Broth

1½ pounds fish bones and trimmings
4 cups cold water
1½ cups dry white wine or water
1 tablespoon lemon juice
1 teaspoon salt
2 teaspoons chopped fresh or ½ teaspoon ground thyme leaves
1 large celery stalk, chopped (about ½ cup)
1 small onion, sliced
3 mushrooms, chopped
2 sprigs parsley
1 bay leaf

Rinse fish bones and trimmings with cold water; drain. Mix bones, trimmings and remaining ingredients in Dutch oven. Heat to boiling; skim foam and reduce heat. Cover and simmer 30 minutes.

Strain through cheesecloth-lined sieve. Discard skin, bones, vegetables and seasonings. Use immediately, or cover and refrigerate up to 24 hours, or freeze for future use.

About 5½ cups broth

PER CUP: Calories 70; Protein 3 g; Carbohydrate 2 g; Fat 0 g; Cholesterol 10 mg; Sodium 420 mg

Broth Basics

When making your own broth, keep these basics in mind:

- No need to peel or trim vegetables; just wash and cut into large pieces.

- To remove particles from strained broth and remove the cloudy appearance, you can clarify the broth. Beat 1 egg white, 1 tablespoon water and 1 broken egg shell. Stir into strained broth. Heat to boiling, stirring constantly. Boil 2 minutes. Remove from heat; let stand 5 minutes. Strain through double-thickness cheesecloth.

- Remember, you can control the salt and spices in your broth. Season to taste by using your favorite spices.

Hot-and-Sour Fish Soup

2 tablespoons cornstarch
2 tablespoons cold water
½ pound fish fillets, cut into 1-inch
   pieces
3 tablespoons white vinegar
2 teaspoons soy sauce
2 medium carrots, cut into thin strips
2 bottles (8 ounces each) clam juice or 2
   cups fish or chicken broth
1 jar (7 ounces) sliced shiitake mushrooms, undrained
1 to 2 teaspoons red pepper sauce
4 ounces fresh Chinese pea pods or 1
   package (6 ounces) frozen Chinese pea
   pods, thawed

Mix cornstarch and cold water. Mix cornstarch mixture and remaining ingredients except pepper sauce and pea pods in 4-quart Dutch oven. Heat to boiling; reduce heat.

Cover and simmer until fish flakes easily with fork, 3 to 5 minutes. Stir in pepper sauce and pea pods. **4 servings**

MICROWAVE DIRECTIONS: Decrease vinegar to 2 tablespoons and use 1 teaspoon red pepper sauce. Coarsely shred carrots. Mix fish, vinegar, soy sauce, carrots, clam juice and mushrooms in 3-quart microwavable casserole. Cover tightly and microwave on high 5 minutes.

Mix cornstarch and cold water; stir into fish mixture. Cover tightly and microwave, stirring every 2 minutes, until mixture thickens and boils, 8 to 10 minutes. Stir in pepper sauce and pea pods. Cover tightly and microwave until pea pods are hot, 1 to 2 minutes.

PER SERVING: Calories 125; Protein 15 g; Carbohydrate 12 g; Fat 2 g; Cholesterol 30 mg; Sodium 780 mg

Catfish Stew

This stew goes well with corn bread, for a southern-inspired meal.

2 medium onions, sliced
1 clove garlic, finely chopped
2 teaspoons chile powder
2 teaspoons vegetable oil
1 can (28 ounces) whole tomatoes,
   undrained
1¾ cups water
½ cup uncooked regular long grain rice
2 teaspoons chopped fresh or ½ teaspoon dried oregano leaves
2 teaspoons chopped fresh or ½ teaspoon dried thyme leaves
½ teaspoon ground cumin
½ teaspoon red pepper sauce
1 package (10 ounces) frozen sliced okra
1 pound catfish or other medium-fat fish
   fillets, cut into 1-inch pieces
½ cup chopped green bell pepper (about
   1 small)

Cook onions, garlic and chile powder in oil in nonstick Dutch oven over medium heat 2 to 3 minutes, stirring occasionally, until onions are softened. Stir in tomatoes, water, rice, oregano, thyme, cumin and pepper sauce; break up tomatoes. Heat to boiling; reduce heat. Cover and simmer 20 minutes.

Rinse okra with cold water to separate; drain. Stir okra, fish and bell pepper into tomato mixture. Heat to boiling; reduce heat. Cover and simmer 5 to 10 minutes, stirring occasionally, until fish flakes easily with fork and okra is done. **6 servings**

PER SERVING: Calories 225; Protein 17 g; Carbohydrate 27 g; Fat 6 g; Cholesterol 45 mg; Sodium 270 mg

Cod–New Potato Soup

2 cups water
½ teaspoon salt
¼ teaspoon pepper
1 small onion, chopped (about ¼ cup)
12 small new potatoes (about 1½
    pounds), cut into fourths
1 stalk celery (with leaves), sliced (about
    ½ cup)
1 pound cod or other lean fish, cut into
    1-inch pieces
1 cup frozen peas
2 cups half-and-half or milk

Heat water, salt, pepper and onion to boiling in Dutch oven. Add potatoes. Heat to boiling; reduce heat. Cover and simmer about 10 minutes or until potatoes are almost done.

Add celery, fish and peas. Heat to boiling; reduce heat. Cover and simmer 6 to 8 minutes, stirring gently after 4 minutes, until fish flakes easily with fork. Stir in half-and-half. Heat until hot. **4 servings**

PER SERVING: Calories 450; Protein 30 g; Carbohydrate 46 g; Fat 16 g; Cholesterol 105 mg; Sodium 460 mg

Fish and Corn Chowder

6 slices bacon, cut into ½-inch pieces
1 pound cod, cut into 1-inch pieces
2 cups water
1 teaspoon salt
¼ teaspoon white pepper
4 new potatoes, cut into ¼-inch slices
2 medium stalks celery, sliced
1 medium onion, chopped
1 can (17 ounces) whole kernel corn,
    undrained
1 cup half-and-half

Cook bacon in 4-quart Dutch oven until crisp; remove bacon and drain. Drain fat from Dutch oven.

Stir remaining ingredients except half-and-half into Dutch oven. Heat to boiling; reduce heat. Cover and simmer until fish and potatoes are done, 15 to 20 minutes. Stir in half-and-half; heat until hot. Sprinkle each serving with bacon and, if desired, garnish with celery leaves.
6 servings

PER SERVING: Calories 270; Protein 19 g; Carbohydrate 32 g; Fat 7 g; Cholesterol 55 mg; Sodium 650 mg

Grouper Soup

If grouper is not available, cod, flounder and scrod also are delicious in this soup.

2 medium onions, chopped (about 1 cup)
2 cloves garlic, crushed
2 tablespoons olive or vegetable oil
1½ pounds grouper or other lean fish fillets, cut into 1-inch pieces
½ teaspoon salt
½ teaspoon dried oregano leaves
½ teaspoon ground red pepper (cayenne)
3 medium tomatoes, coarsely chopped (about 3 cups)
2 medium green bell peppers, chopped (about 2 cups)
2 cans (10¾ ounces each) condensed chicken broth
2 broth cans water

Cook onions and garlic in oil in Dutch oven, stirring frequently, until onions are softened. Stir in remaining ingredients. Heat to boiling; reduce heat. Cover and simmer about 5 minutes or until fish flakes easily with fork.   **8 servings**

PER SERVING: Calories 225; Protein 28 g; Carbohydrate 7 g; Fat 9 g; Cholesterol 45 mg; Sodium 710 mg

Salmon-Potato Soup

2 cups chicken broth
½ teaspoon dry mustard
¼ teaspoon pepper
1 medium onion, sliced and separated into rings
1½ pounds new potatoes (10 to 12), cut into ½-inch slices
1 pound salmon or other fatty fish fillets, skinned and cut into 4 serving pieces*
1 cup half-and-half
4 teaspoons chopped fresh parsley

Heat broth, mustard and pepper to boiling in Dutch oven. Add the onion and potatoes. Arrange salmon on potatoes. Heat to boiling; reduce heat. Cover and simmer 10 to 15 minutes or until fish flakes easily with fork and potatoes are tender.

Pour half-and-half into Dutch oven. Heat until hot. Serve soup in shallow bowls, placing 1 piece of salmon in each bowl. Sprinkle each serving with 1 teaspoon parsley. Serve with cracked black pepper if desired.

4 servings

1 can (14¾ ounces) salmon, drained and flaked, can be substituted for the salmon fillets. Arrange over potatoes just before adding half-and-half.

PER SERVING: Calories 390; Protein 28 g; Carbohydrate 37 g; Fat 14 g; Cholesterol 80 mg; Sodium 470 mg

Cream of Smoked Salmon Soup

1 package (8 ounces) cream cheese, cut into cubes
1 cup milk
2 teaspoons Dijon mustard
1½ teaspoons chopped fresh or ½ teaspoon dried dill weed
2 green onions (with tops), sliced
1 can (14½ ounces) chicken broth
12 ounces smoked salmon, flaked*

Heat cream cheese, milk, mustard, dill weed, onions and chicken broth in 2-quart saucepan over medium heat until cheese is melted and mixture is smooth. Stir in salmon. Heat until hot. **4 servings**

MICROWAVE DIRECTIONS: Place all ingredients except salmon in 2-quart microwavable casserole. Cover tightly and microwave on high 8 to 10 minutes, stirring every 2 minutes, until cheese is melted. Stir in salmon. Cover tightly and microwave 2 minutes longer.

1 can (15½ ounces) salmon, drained and flaked, can be substituted for the smoked salmon.

PER SERVING: Calories 380; Protein 26 g; Carbohydrate 6 g; Fat 28 g; Cholesterol 70 mg; Sodium 860 mg

Red Snapper and Celery Cabbage Soup

Celery cabbage is known by many names, such as Napa cabbage, Chinese cabbage and Peking cabbage.

½ pound skinless red snapper, sea bass or other lean fish fillets
1 teaspoon cornstarch
1 teaspoon finely chopped gingerroot or ¼ teaspoon ground ginger
1 teaspoon vegetable oil
1 teaspoon sesame oil
½ teaspoon salt
½ teaspoon light soy sauce
⅛ teaspoon white pepper
8 ounces celery cabbage
4 cups chicken broth
1 teaspoon sesame oil
2 tablespoons chopped green onions with tops (about 1 medium)

Cut fish fillets crosswise into ½-inch slices. Toss fish, cornstarch, gingerroot, vegetable oil, 1 teaspoon sesame oil, the salt, soy sauce and white pepper in medium bowl. Cover and refrigerate 30 minutes. Cut celery cabbage into ½-inch slices.

Heat broth to boiling in 3-quart saucepan. Add celery cabbage. Heat to boiling; stir in fish mixture. Heat to boiling; reduce heat to medium. Simmer uncovered 2 minutes; remove from heat. Stir in 1 teaspoon sesame oil and the onions. **4 servings**

PER SERVING: Calories 140; Protein 17 g; Carbohydrate 4 g; Fat 6 g; Cholesterol 20 mg; Sodium 1160 mg

Red Snapper Stew

1 medium onion, sliced
1 tablespoon reduced-calorie margarine
4 cups chicken broth
1 cup ¼-inch slices carrots (about 2 medium)
½ cup uncooked regular rice
1 tablespoon lemon juice
½ teaspoon salt
¼ teaspoon dried dill weed
1 teaspoon chopped fresh or ¼ teaspoon dried thyme leaves
¼ teaspoon pepper
1 package (10 ounces) frozen baby Brussels sprouts
1½ pounds red snapper or other lean fish fillets, cut into 1-inch pieces
1 cup sliced mushrooms (about 3 ounces)

Cook and stir onion in margarine in Dutch oven over medium heat until onion is softened, about 5 minutes. Stir in broth, carrots, rice, lemon juice, salt, dill weed, thyme and pepper. Heat to boiling; reduce heat. Cover and simmer until rice is tender, about 20 minutes.

Rinse Brussels sprouts under running cold water to separate; drain. Stir into rice mixture. Heat to boiling; reduce heat. Simmer uncovered 5 minutes. Stir in fish and mushrooms; simmer until fish flakes easily with fork, 5 to 8 minutes longer. **4 servings**

PER SERVING: Calories 320; Protein 33 g; Carbohydrate 33 g; Fat 6 g; Cholesterol 40 mg; Sodium 1160 mg

New England Clam Chowder

Clam chowder has been popular since colonial days, and the original recipe called for cream and clams, the classic New England clam chowder.

¼ cup cut-up bacon or lean salt pork
1 medium onion, chopped (about ½ cup)
2 cans (8 ounces each) minced or whole clams*
1 cup finely chopped potato
½ teaspoon salt
Dash of pepper
2 cups milk

Cook and stir bacon and onion in 2-quart saucepan over medium heat until bacon is crisp and onion is softened. Drain clams, reserving liquor. Add enough water, if necessary, to clam liquor to measure 1 cup. Stir clams, clam liquor, potato, salt and pepper into bacon and onion. Heat to boiling; reduce heat. Cover and simmer about 15 minutes or until potato is tender. Stir in milk. Heat, stirring occasionally, just until hot (do not boil). **4 servings**

*1 pint shucked fresh clams with liquor can be substituted for the canned clams. Chop clams and stir in with the potatoes.

PER SERVING: Calories 345; Protein 22 g; Carbohydrate 22 g; Fat 19 g; Cholesterol 25 mg; Sodium 1180 mg

Manhattan Clam Chowder

To a New Englander, Manhattan Clam Chowder is heresy in a bowl: Water is used instead of the milk found in the New England version. Here, luscious tomatoes simmer along with the clams.

- ¼ cup finely cut-up bacon or salt pork
- 1 small onion, finely chopped (about ¼ cup)
- 1 pint shucked fresh clams* (reserve liquor)
- 2 cups finely chopped pared potatoes
- ⅓ cup chopped celery
- 1 cup water
- 2 teaspoons chopped fresh parsley
- 1 teaspoon chopped fresh or ¼ teaspoon dried thyme leaves
- ½ teaspoon salt
- ⅛ teaspoon pepper
- 1 can (16 ounces) tomatoes, undrained

Cook and stir bacon and onion in Dutch oven over medium heat until bacon is crisp and onion is softened. Drain and chop clams, reserving liquor. Stir clams, clam liquor, potatoes, celery and water into bacon mixture. Heat to boiling; reduce heat. Cover and cook about 10 minutes or until potatoes are tender. Stir in remaining ingredients. Heat to boiling, stirring occasionally. **4 to 6 servings**

2 cans (6½ ounces each) minced or whole clams can be substituted for the fresh clams. Stir in clams with the potatoes.

PER SERVING: Calories 225; Protein 21 g; Carbohydrate 26 g; Fat 4 g; Cholesterol 50 mg; Sodium 620 mg

Vegetable Clam Chowder

Frozen vegetables and canned clams make this tasty chowder super easy!

- 2 tablespoons margarine or butter
- 1 package (16 ounces) frozen broccoli, corn and red peppers
- 2 cans (6½ ounces each) minced clams, drained
- 3 cups milk
- 1 teaspoon salt
- ⅛ teaspoon pepper

Place margarine and frozen vegetables in 3-quart microwavable casserole. Cover tightly and microwave on high 8 to 10 minutes or until hot. Stir in remaining ingredients. Cover tightly and microwave on medium-high (70%) 10 to 12 minutes, stirring after 5 minutes, until hot. **4 servings**

PER SERVING: Calories 235; Protein 14 g; Carbohydrate 23 g; Fat 10 g; Cholesterol 30 mg; Sodium 74 mg

Lobster Bisque

Bisques are thick, rich soups, generally showcasing seafood, and this lobster version is just right for a special dinner.

1 small onion, finely chopped (about ¼ cup)
3 tablespoons butter or margarine
3 tablespoons all-purpose flour
1 tablespoon chopped fresh parsley
½ teaspoon salt
⅛ teaspoon pepper
2 cups milk
1 cup water or chicken broth
1¼ cups chopped fresh or frozen (thawed) lobster (about 12 ounces)

Cook and stir onion in butter in 3-quart saucepan over low heat until onion is softened. Stir in flour, parsley, salt and pepper. Cook, stirring constantly, until mixture is bubbly; remove from heat. Stir in milk and water. Heat to boiling, stirring constantly. Boil and stir 1 minute. Stir in lobster. Heat to boiling; reduce heat. Cook about 3 minutes, stirring frequently, until lobster is white. **4 servings**

PER SERVING: Calories 205; Protein 14 g; Carbohydrate 12 g; Fat 11 g; Cholesterol 65 mg; Sodium 560 mg

Removing Lobster Meat

Place the lobster on its back. Using kitchen scissors, cut lengthwise down the body up to the tail, cutting to but not through, the back shell.

Cut away the membrane on the tail to expose meat. Discard the intestinal vein running through the tail and the small sac near the head of the lobster. You can serve the green tomalley (liver) and coral roe (only in females) if you like.

Twist the large claws away from the body of the lobster. Using a nutcracker, break open the claws. Remove meat from claws, tail and body.

Oyster and Vegetable Chowder

⅓ cup margarine or butter
1½ pints shucked select or large oysters, undrained*
1 package (16 ounces) frozen corn-broccoli mixture
3½ cups milk
1½ teaspoons salt
Dash of pepper

Heat margarine in 3-quart saucepan until melted. Stir in oysters and vegetables. Cook over medium heat, stirring frequently, until edges of oysters are curled and vegetables are done, about 14 minutes.

Stir in milk, salt and pepper. Cook over low heat, stirring frequently, until hot. **6 servings**

PER SERVING: Calories 350; Protein 23 g; Carbohydrate 21 g; Fat 19 g; Cholesterol 140 mg; Sodium 1010 mg

3 cans (8 ounces each) whole oysters, undrained, can be substituted for fresh oysters; stir in with the milk.

Oyster and Vegetable Chowder

Scallop and Shrimp Minestrone

2 cups chopped onions (about 2 large)
½ cup chopped carrot (about 1 medium)
1 cup chicken broth
1 clove garlic, finely chopped
1½ cups tomato juice
2 tablespoons lemon juice
1 can (14½ ounces) whole tomatoes,
   undrained
1 bay leaf
½ cup uncooked medium pasta shells
1 cup chopped mushrooms (about 4
   ounces)
½ cup chopped yellow summer squash
½ cup chopped zucchini
2 tablespoons chopped fresh parsley
¼ teaspoon salt
¼ teaspoon pepper
12 raw large shrimp, peeled and de-
   veined (about ¾ pound)
6 ounces sea scallops

Cook onions, carrots, broth and garlic in 2-quart saucepan over medium heat 5 minutes, stirring occasionally. Stir in tomato juice, lemon juice, tomatoes and bay leaf; break up tomatoes. Reduce heat. Simmer covered 10 minutes.

Stir in pasta. Cook 7 minutes. Stir in remaining ingredients. Cover and cook 5 minutes, stirring occasionally, until shrimp are pink.

6 servings

PER SERVING: Calories 180; Protein 17 g; Carbohydrate 23 g; Fat 2 g; Cholesterol 65 mg; Sodium 690 mg

Oyster Soup

¼ cup (½ stick) margarine or butter
1 pint shucked oysters, undrained
2 cups milk
½ cup half-and-half
½ teaspoon salt
Dash of pepper

Heat margarine in 1½-quart saucepan until melted. Add oysters. Cook and stir over low heat just until edges curl. Heat milk and half-and-half in 2-quart saucepan. Stir in salt, pepper and oysters.

4 servings

PER SERVING: Calories 260; Protein 12 g; Carbohydrate 10 g; Fat 19 g; Cholesterol 65 mg; Sodium 408 mg

Avocado-Crab Soup

1 can (10¾ ounces) condensed chicken
   broth
1 cup water
1 green onion (with top), cut into about
   1-inch pieces
1 small clove garlic
1 tablespoon lemon juice
2 medium avocados, pared and cut up
1 cup plain yogurt
1 package (6 ounces) frozen crabmeat,
   thawed*

Heat chicken broth, water, green onion and garlic to boiling in 2-quart saucepan. Pour hot mixture into food processor or blender. Add lemon juice and avocados. Cover and process or blend about 30 seconds or until smooth.

Pour mixture back into saucepan. Stir in yogurt and crabmeat. Heat, stirring constantly, just until hot.

4 servings

1 can (6 ounces) crabmeat, drained, or 1 package (8 ounces) salad-style imitation crabmeat can be substituted for the frozen crabmeat.

PER SERVING: Calories 245; Protein 15 g; Carbohydrate 12 g; Fat 15 g; Cholesterol 45 mg; Sodium 410 mg

Avocado-Crab Soup

Shrimp-Tofu Ball Soup

Shrimp-Tofu Ball Soup

Tofu is the Japanese word for bean curd, a wonderful source of cholesterol-free protein. In itself mild in flavor, tofu readily absorbs the tastes of any ingredients with which it is cooked. The shrimp balls in this soup are rather delicate so you may want to use a spoon to place them gently in the broth.

12 Chinese pea pods
6 ounces firm tofu
½ pound raw medium shrimp (in shells)
1 egg white
1 tablespoon cornstarch
⅛ teaspoon white pepper
1 teaspoon sesame oil
1 teaspoon vegetable oil
1 teaspoon salt
4 cups chicken broth
1 teaspoon salt
1 green onion (with top), chopped

Remove strings from pea pods; cut pea pods diagonally into halves. Rinse tofu under cold water; drain. Mash tofu with a fork.

Peel shrimp. Make a shallow cut lengthwise down back of each shrimp; wash out vein. Chop shrimp finely. Mix shrimp, tofu, egg white, cornstarch, white pepper, sesame oil, vegetable oil and 1 teaspoon salt. Shape shrimp mixture into 1-inch balls.

Heat broth and 1 teaspoon salt to boiling in 2-quart saucepan. Add shrimp balls to broth; heat to boiling. Add pea pods; boil 1 minute. Remove from heat; stir in green onion.

4 to 5 servings

PER SERVING: Calories 170; Protein 19 g; Carbohydrate 5 g; Fat 8 g; Cholesterol 55 mg; Sodium 1920 mg

Shrimp Gumbo

Creole cooks in Louisiana invented gumbo. Filé powder, made from dried, pulverized sassafras leaves, must be added at the end of the cooking time; otherwise it becomes stringy.

2 cloves garlic, finely chopped
2 medium onions, sliced
½ medium green bell pepper, thinly sliced
2 tablespoons butter or margarine
12 ounces fresh okra, cut into ½-inch pieces*
1 can (16 ounces) tomatoes, undrained
1 can (6 ounces) tomato paste
3 cups beef broth
1 tablespoon Worcestershire sauce
1 teaspoon salt
1 teaspoon chile powder
1 teaspoon chopped fresh or ½ teaspoon dried basil leaves
¼ teaspoon pepper
1 bay leaf
1½ pounds cleaned raw shrimp**
1 tablespoon filé powder
3 cups hot cooked rice

Cook and stir garlic, onions and bell pepper in butter in Dutch oven over medium heat until tender. Stir in okra, tomatoes, tomato paste, broth, Worcestershire sauce, salt, chile powder, basil, pepper and bay leaf. Break up tomatoes with fork. Heat to boiling; reduce heat. Simmer uncovered 45 minutes. Stir in shrimp. Cover and simmer 5 minutes or until shrimp are pink and tender. Remove bay leaf; stir in filé powder. Serve with hot cooked rice. **8 servings**

*1 package (10 ounces) frozen okra may be substituted for the fresh okra.
**About 1¾ pounds fresh or frozen raw shrimp in shells.

PER SERVING: Calories 250; Protein 19 g; Carbohydrate 35 g; Fat 4 g; Cholesterol 130 mg; Sodium 1240 mg

Bouillabaisse

Bouillabaisse

Serve lots of crusty French bread to mop up the flavorful broth or ladle the soup directly over a thick slice of toasted, crusty bread.

1 cup chopped onion
¼ cup chopped carrot
1 clove garlic, finely chopped
½ cup vegetable oil
3 pounds frozen fish fillets, thawed and cut into 3-inch pieces
1 can (16 ounces) whole tomatoes, undrained
2 bay leaves
2 quarts water
1 pound fresh or frozen shelled raw shrimp
½ cup chopped pimiento
¼ cup chopped fresh parsley
1 tablespoon salt
1 tablespoon lemon juice
½ teaspoon saffron
Dash of pepper
6 fresh or frozen lobster tails, cut lengthwise into halves
1 can (10½ ounces) beef broth

Cook and stir onion, carrot and garlic in vegetable oil in Dutch oven over medium heat about 10 minutes or until onion is softened. Add fish, tomatoes, bay leaves and water. Heat to boiling; reduce heat. Cover and simmer 30 minutes. Stir in remaining ingredients; cover and simmer 30 minutes. Remove bay leaves. Serve in large bowls with French bread if desired.

10 servings

PER SERVING: Calories 360; Protein 51 g; Carbohydrate 7 g; Fat 14 g; Cholesterol 190 mg; Sodium 1240 mg

Baja Seafood Stew

1 medium onion, chopped (about ½ cup)
½ cup chopped green chiles
2 cloves garlic, finely chopped
¼ cup olive oil
2 cups dry white wine, clam juice or water
1½ cups orange juice
1 tablespoon grated orange peel
1 tablespoon sugar
1 tablespoon chopped fresh cilantro
1 teaspoon dried basil leaves
1 teaspoon salt
½ teaspoon pepper
½ teaspoon dried oregano leaves
1 can (28 ounces) whole Italian pear-shaped tomatoes, undrained and cut into halves
24 soft-shell clams (steamers), scrubbed
1½ pounds shelled medium raw shrimp
1 pound cod, sea bass, mahimahi or red snapper fillets, cut into 1-inch pieces
1 package (6 ounces) frozen crabmeat, thawed, drained and cartilage removed

Cook and stir onion, chiles, and garlic in oil in 6-quart Dutch oven over medium heat until onion is softened. Stir in remaining ingredients except the seafood. Heat to boiling; reduce heat. Simmer uncovered 15 minutes.

Add clams; cover and simmer until clams open, 5 to 10 minutes. (Discard any clams that have not opened.) Carefully stir in shrimp, cod and crabmeat. Heat to boiling; reduce heat. Cover and simmer until shrimp are pink and cod flakes easily with fork, 4 to 5 minutes.

6 to 8 servings

PER SERVING: Calories 405; Protein 50 g; Carbohydrate 22 g; Fat 13 g; Cholesterol 260 mg; Sodium 960 mg

Zuni Vegetable Stew (page 60)

4

Hearty Meatless Soups and Stews

Finnish Summer Vegetable Soup

Serve this summer soup with rye bread and some cheese for a satisfying lunch.

2 cups water
2 small carrots, sliced
1 medium potato, cubed
¾ cup fresh or frozen green peas
1 cup cut fresh or frozen green beans
¼ small cauliflower, separated into flowerets
2 ounces fresh spinach, cut up (about 2 cups)
2 cups milk
2 tablespoons all-purpose flour
¼ cup whipping (heavy) cream
1½ teaspoons salt
⅛ teaspoon pepper
Chopped dill weed or parsley, if desired

Heat water, carrots, potato, peas, beans and cauliflower to boiling in 3-quart saucepan; reduce heat. Cover and simmer until vegetables are almost tender, 10 to 15 minutes.

Add spinach; cook uncovered about 1 minute. Mix ¼ cup of the milk and the flour; stir gradually into vegetable mixture. Boil and stir 1 minute. Stir in remaining milk, the whipping cream, salt and pepper. Heat just until hot. Garnish each serving with dill weed. **10 servings**

PER SERVING: Calories 85; Protein 3 g; Carbohydrate 11 g; Fat 3 g; Cholesterol 10 mg; Sodium 380 mg

Vegetable-Cheese Soup

½ cup finely chopped carrots
½ cup finely chopped celery
2 large potatoes, finely chopped
2 large onions, finely chopped
2 cans (12 ounces each) beer or 3 cups
    water
4 teaspoons chicken bouillon granules
2 cups shredded Cheddar or process
    American cheese (about 8 ounces)
1 cup half-and-half
⅛ teaspoon ground nutmeg
6 drops red pepper sauce
¼ cup chopped parsley

Heat vegetables, beer and bouillon granules to boiling in 3-quart saucepan; reduce heat. Cover and simmer until vegetables are tender, about 15 minutes. Stir in remaining ingredients except parsley; heat through. Sprinkle with parsley.

6 to 8 servings

PER SERVING: Calories 325; Protein 13 g; Carbohydrate 28 g; Fat 18 g; Cholesterol 55 mg; Sodium 1130 mg

Pasta Magic

Make any soup a pasta soup. For canned or dry mix soups, precook pasta and add just before serving. If making homemade soup, add during the last 15 minutes of cooking.

Zuni Vegetable Stew

The Zuni, a tribe of Pueblo Indians, live in New Mexico. The fresh ingredients that make up this hearty stew (various chiles and squashes, corn and beans) are representative of that region's native bounty.

¾ cup chopped onion
1 clove garlic, finely chopped
2 tablespoons vegetable oil
1 large red bell pepper, cut into 2 × ½-
    inch strips
2 medium poblano or Anaheim chiles,
    seeded and cut into 2 × ½-inch strips
1 jalapeño chile, seeded and chopped
1 cup cubed Hubbard or acorn squash
    (about ½ pound)
2 cans (14½ ounces each) chicken broth
½ teaspoon salt
½ teaspoon pepper
½ teaspoon ground coriander
1 cup thinly sliced zucchini
1 cup thinly sliced yellow squash
1 can (17 ounces) whole kernel corn,
    drained
1 can (16 ounces) pinto beans, drained

Cook and stir onion and garlic in oil in 4-quart Dutch oven over medium heat until onion is softened. Stir in bell pepper, poblano and jalapeño chiles. Cook 15 minutes.

Stir in Hubbard squash, broth, salt, pepper and coriander. Heat to boiling; reduce heat. Cover and simmer until squash is tender, about 15 minutes. Stir in remaining ingredients. Cook uncovered, stirring occasionally, until zucchini is tender, about 10 minutes. **6 servings**

PER SERVING: Calories 245; Protein 10 g; Carbohydrate 35 g; Fat 7 g; Cholesterol 0 mg; Sodium 900 mg

Shredded Cabbage Soup

Here is a hearty Russian soup, tradition-ally enriched with a dollop of sour cream just before serving.

2 medium onions, thinly sliced
3 tablespoons bacon fat, margarine or butter
2 cans (10½ ounces each) condensed beef broth
2 broth cans water
1 small head green cabbage, coarsely shredded (5 cups)
2 medium carrots, sliced
2 medium potatoes, cubed
1 stalk celery (with leaves), sliced
2 medium tomatoes, coarsely chopped
1 teaspoon salt
Freshly ground pepper
Sour cream
Dill weed or parsley, if desired

Cook and stir onions in bacon fat in Dutch oven over medium heat until softened. Add beef broth, water, cabbage, carrots, potatoes and celery. Heat to boiling; reduce heat. Cover and simmer until vegetables are tender, about 20 minutes. Stir in tomatoes, salt and pepper. Simmer uncovered about 10 minutes. Top each serving with sour cream. Garnish with dill weed. **12 servings**

PER SERVING: Calories 120; Protein 3 g; Carbohydrate 13 g; Fat 6 g; Cholesterol 20 mg; Sodium 360 mg

Lentil and Brown Rice Soup

¾ cup dried lentils
½ cup uncooked brown or regular rice
6 cups water
½ teaspoon ground cumin
½ teaspoon salt
¼ teaspoon pepper
½ package (2.5-ounce size) onion soup mix (1 envelope)
3 ounces spinach, cut into ½-inch strips (about 1 cup)
2 tablespoons snipped cilantro or parsley
3 tablespoons lemon juice

Heat lentils, rice, water, cumin, salt, pepper and soup mix (dry) to boiling in 4-quart Dutch oven; reduce heat. Cover and simmer, stirring occasionally, until lentils are tender, about 40 minutes.

Stir in spinach, cilantro and lemon juice until spinach is wilted. Serve with additional snipped cilantro and lemon slices if desired.

4 servings

PER SERVING: Calories 250; Protein 13 g; Carbohydrate 45 g; Fat 2 g; Cholesterol 450 mg; Sodium 1080 mg

Cream of Lettuce Soup

Make this fresh-flavored French soup when tender lettuces are in abundance at the market.

1 small onion, chopped
¼ cup margarine or butter
2 large heads Boston lettuce or 2 small bunches romaine, finely shredded (about 7 cups)
¼ cup all-purpose flour
3 cups water
1 tablespoon chicken bouillon granules
1 cup half-and-half
½ teaspoon salt
⅛ teaspoon pepper
Mint leaves or parsley

Cook and stir onion in margarine in 3-quart saucepan over low heat until softened. Reserve 1 cup lettuce; stir remaining lettuce into onion. Cover and cook over low heat until lettuce wilts, about 5 minutes. Stir in flour; cook and stir 1 minute. Add water and bouillon. Heat to boiling, stirring constantly. Boil and stir 1 minute.

Pour mixture into blender container. Cover and blend on high speed until smooth, about 30 seconds; pour into saucepan. Stir in reserved lettuce, the half-and-half, salt and pepper. Heat just to boiling. Garnish with mint.

6 servings

PER SERVING: Calories 165; Protein 3 g; Carbohydrate 9 g; Fat 13 g; Cholesterol 15 mg; Sodium 930 mg

Golden Onion Soup

Parmesan Croutons (below)
¼ cup margarine or butter
1 tablespoon packed brown sugar
1 teaspoon Worcestershire sauce
2 large onions (about ¾ pound each), cut into fourths and sliced
2 cans (10½ ounces each) condensed chicken or beef broth
2 soup cans water

Prepare Parmesan Croutons; reserve. Reduce oven temperature to 325°. Heat margarine in Dutch oven until melted. Stir in brown sugar and Worcestershire sauce. Toss onions in margarine mixture.

Bake uncovered about 2½ hours, stirring every hour, until onions are deep golden brown. Stir in broth and water. Heat to boiling over high heat. Serve with Parmesan Croutons.

6 servings

Parmesan Croutons

¼ cup margarine or butter
3 slices bread, cut into 1-inch cubes
Grated Parmesan cheese

Heat oven to 400°. Heat margarine in rectangular pan, 13×9×2 inches, in oven until melted. Toss bread cubes in margarine until evenly coated. Sprinkle with cheese. Bake uncovered 10 to 15 minutes, stirring occasionally, until golden brown and crisp. **6 servings**

PER SERVING: Calories 265; Protein 8 g; Carbohydrate 21 g; Fat 17 g; Cholesterol 5 mg; Sodium 960 mg

Cream of Broccoli Soup

1½ pounds broccoli
2 tablespoons butter
2 cloves garlic, finely chopped
1 small onion, finely chopped
3 cups whipping (heavy) cream
2 tablespoons lemon juice
2 medium stalks celery, chopped
2 bay leaves
1 can (14½ ounces) chicken broth
3 cups milk
2 tablespoons chopped fresh parsley
1 teaspoon ground sage or freshly
    grated nutmeg
½ teaspoon pepper
2 tablespoons freshly grated Parmesan
    cheese

Cut broccoli flowerets from stems; reserve. Chop broccoli stems. Heat butter in 4-quart Dutch oven over medium-high heat. Sauté garlic and onion in butter. Stir in broccoli stems, whipping cream, lemon juice, celery, bay leaves and broth. Heat to boiling. Boil uncovered 15 minutes; reduce heat to medium. Stir in broccoli flowerets, milk, parsley, sage and pepper. Cover and cook 30 minutes. Remove bay leaves. Top each serving with cheese.   **12 servings**

PER SERVING: Calories 260; Protein 6 g; Carbohydrate 9 g; Fat 22 g; Cholesterol 75 mg; Sodium 210 mg

Cream of Spinach Soup

This creamy soup would make a lovely first course or be welcomed as a light lunch.

2 tablespoons olive oil
2 tablespoons butter
2 tablespoons chopped fresh parsley
4 cloves garlic, finely chopped
1 leek, thinly sliced
1 pound fresh spinach, torn into bite-size
    pieces
2 cups whipping (heavy) cream
2 cups milk
2 cups chicken broth
1 tablespoon lemon juice
1 teaspoon freshly grated nutmeg
1 teaspoon salt
½ teaspoon white pepper

Heat oil and butter in 4-quart Dutch oven over medium-high heat. Sauté parsley, garlic and leek in oil mixture. Add spinach; cook uncovered over low heat 10 minutes, stirring frequently. Stir in whipping cream, milk, chicken broth and lemon juice. Heat to boiling; reduce heat. Cover and simmer 1 hour, stirring occasionally. Stir in remaining ingredients.   **6 servings**

PER SERVING: Calories 395; Protein 8 g; Carbohydrate 12 g; Fat 35 g; Cholesterol 105 mg; Sodium 750 mg

Apple and Squash Bisque

1 can (14½ ounces) chicken broth
1 butternut squash* (about 2 pounds),
   pared and cubed
½ cup chopped onion
2 cups applesauce
½ teaspoon ground ginger
¼ teaspoon salt
1 cup sour cream

Heat chicken broth to boiling in 3-quart sauce-pan; add squash and onion. Cover and heat to boiling; reduce heat. Boil 15 to 20 minutes or until squash is tender. Stir in applesauce, ginger and salt. Place one-third to one-half of the mix-ture at a time in blender or food processor. Cover and blend or process until smooth. Return soup to saucepan; stir in sour cream. Heat over low heat, stirring occasionally, until hot. Garnish with additional sour cream and sprinkle with poppy seed, if desired. **6 servings**

MICROWAVE DIRECTIONS: Place chicken broth, squash and onion in 3-quart microwavable cas-serole. Cover tightly and microwave on high 13 to 16 minutes, stirring after 5 minutes, until tender. Stir in applesauce, ginger, and salt. Blend as directed above. Return soup to casse-role; stir in sour cream. Microwave uncovered on medium-high (70%) 6 to 8 minutes, stirring every 2 minutes, until hot.

*2 packages (10 ounces each) frozen squash, thawed, can be substituted for the butternut squash.

PER SERVING: Calories 220; Protein 4 g; Carbohy-drate 30 g; Fat 9 g; Cholesterol 25 mg; Sodium 330 mg

Butternut Squash Soup

To toast nuts, spread them in a single layer in an ungreased pan; bake at 350°, stirring and checking for doneness fre-quently. Nuts are toasted when they are lightly browned.

1 medium onion, chopped (about ½ cup)
2 tablespoons margarine or butter
2 cups chicken broth
1 pound butternut squash, pared, seeded
   and cut into 1-inch cubes
2 pears, pared and sliced
1 teaspoon chopped fresh thyme leaves
¼ teaspoon salt
¼ teaspoon white pepper
¼ teaspoon ground coriander
1 cup whipping (heavy) cream
1 unpared pear, sliced
½ cup chopped pecans, toasted

Cook and stir onion in margarine in 4-quart Dutch oven over medium heat until softened. Stir in broth, squash, 2 sliced pears, thyme, salt, white pepper and coriander. Heat to boiling; re-duce heat. Cover and simmer until squash is tender, 10 to 15 minutes.

Pour about half of the soup into blender or food processor; cover and blend or process until smooth. Repeat with remaining soup. Return to Dutch oven; stir in whipping cream. Heat, stirring frequently, until hot. Serve with sliced pear and pecans. **6 servings**

PER SERVING: Calories 310; Protein 4 g; Carbohy-drate 19 g; Fat 24 g; Cholesterol 45 mg; Sodium 480 mg

Butternut Squash Soup

Chunky Tomato Soup

2 tablespoons olive oil
4 cloves garlic, chopped
2 medium stalks celery, coarsely
  chopped
2 medium carrots, coarsely chopped
2 cans (28 ounces each) Italian pear-
  shaped tomatoes, undrained
4 cups water
2 cans (14½ ounces each) chicken broth
1 teaspoon dried basil
½ teaspoon pepper
2 bay leaves
8 slices hard-crusted Italian bread, each
  1 inch thick

Heat oil in 4-quart Dutch oven over medium-high heat. Sauté garlic, celery and carrots in oil. Stir in tomatoes; break up tomatoes coarsely. Stir in water, broth, basil, pepper and bay leaves. Heat to boiling; reduce heat. Cover and simmer 1 hour, stirring occasionally. Remove bay leaves.

Heat oven to 425°. Place bread on ungreased cookie sheet. Toast bread, turning once, until deep golden brown, about 6 minutes. Place 1 slice toast in each of 8 bowls. Ladle soup over toast; serve immediately. **8 servings**

PER SERVING: Calories 190; Protein 7 g; Carbohydrate 29 g; Fat 5 g; Cholesterol 0 mg; Sodium 850 mg

Tomato Soup with Dill

Try floating bagel chips in this fresh soup for a delicious crunch.

3 tablespoons margarine or butter
2 medium onions, finely chopped (about
  1 cup)
2 large carrots, peeled and finely
  chopped
2 cloves garlic, crushed
3 cups chicken broth
¾ teaspoon salt
½ teaspoon pepper
12 ripe medium tomatoes, seeded and
  diced (about 8 cups)
1 cup half-and-half
½ cup chopped fresh dill weed

Melt margarine in Dutch oven over medium heat. Cook and stir onions, carrots and garlic 5 minutes or until vegetables are soft. Add remaining ingredients except half-and-half and dill weed. Cook, uncovered, over medium heat 40 minutes, stirring occasionally. Cool slightly.

Place soup in blender or food processor; cover and blend or process until smooth. Stir in half-and-half. Keep soup hot until ready to serve. Serve with chopped dill weed. **4 servings**

PER SERVING: Calories 355; Protein 11 g; Carbohydrates 37 g; Fat 18 g; Cholesterol 25 mg; Sodium 1190 mg

Tomato Egg Drop Soup

Stir-fried onion, tomato and black mushrooms add color, texture and flavor to classic Egg Drop Soup. Garnish with sprigs of cilantro; it complements the tomato flavor.

6 dried black mushrooms
1 large tomato
4 cups chicken broth
1 tablespoon vegetable oil
1 small onion, sliced
2 eggs
1 teaspoon salt
½ teaspoon white pepper

Soak mushrooms in hot water 20 minutes or until soft; drain. Rinse in warm water; drain. Squeeze out excess moisture. Remove and discard stems; cut caps into thin strips. Place tomato in boiling water; boil 10 seconds. Immediately place in cold water. Peel; cut into 8 wedges; cut each wedge into halves.

Heat broth to boiling in 3-quart saucepan. Heat wok until hot. Add vegetable oil; tilt wok to coat side. Add onion; stir-fry 1 minute. Add mushrooms and tomato; stir-fry 2 minutes.

Stir tomato mixture into broth; reduce heat to medium. Cover and simmer 5 minutes. Heat to rolling boil over high heat. (If broth is not heated to a rolling boil, egg will not form threads.)

Mix eggs, salt and white pepper. Pour egg mixture slowly into broth, stirring constantly with fork, until egg forms threads.

4 to 5 servings

PER SERVING: Calories 135; Protein 9 g; Carbohydrate 7 g; Fat 8 g; Cholesterol 105 mg; Sodium 1340 mg

Zucchini Soup

Zucchini, low in calories, is a plentiful plant for home gardeners and is readily available year 'round.

¼ cup chopped onion (about 1 small)
1 tablespoon reduced-calorie margarine
2 cups chicken broth
2 tablespoons finely chopped canned green chiles
½ teaspoon salt
⅛ teaspoon pepper
2 cups chopped zucchini (about 2 small)
1 can (8¾ ounces) whole kernel corn, drained
1 cup milk
2 ounces Monterey Jack cheese, cut into ¼-inch cubes (½ cup)
Ground nutmeg
Chopped fresh parsley

Cook onion in margarine in 2-quart saucepan, stirring occasionally, until onion is softened. Stir in broth, chiles, salt, pepper, zucchini and corn. Heat to boiling; reduce heat. Cover and simmer about 5 minutes or until zucchini is tender. Stir in milk; heat until hot. Stir in cheese. Garnish with nutmeg and parsley. **4 servings**

PER SERVING: Calories 205; Protein 10 g; Carbohydrate 19 g; Fat 10 g; Cholesterol 20 mg; Sodium 820 mg

Minestrone with Pesto

Minestrone with Pesto

Pesto adds extra flavor to this Italian favorite.

4 cups raw vegetable pieces*
½ teaspoon dried basil leaves
⅛ teaspoon pepper
1 medium onion, chopped
1 clove garlic, finely chopped
1 can (15 ounces) kidney or garbanzo beans, undrained
2 cans (10½ ounces each) condensed chicken or beef broth
2 broth cans water
2 ounces uncooked spaghetti, broken into 2- to 3-inch pieces, or ½ cup uncooked macaroni
5 ounces spinach, cut crosswise into ¼-inch strips
Pesto (below) or prepared pesto

Heat all ingredients except spinach and Pesto to boiling in 4-quart Dutch oven; reduce heat.

Cover and simmer until vegetables and spaghetti are tender, about 10 minutes. Stir in spinach until wilted. Serve with Pesto and, if desired, grated Parmesan cheese.   **6 servings**

*Sliced carrots, celery, zucchini or yellow summer squash, green or yellow beans, cut into 1-inch slices, chopped tomatoes or shelled peas can be used.

PER SERVING: Calories 205; Protein 10 g; Carbohydrate 28 g; Fat 6 g; Cholesterol 5 mg; Sodium 530 mg

Pesto

2 cups firmly packed chopped fresh basil leaves
¾ cup grated Parmesan cheese
¾ cup olive oil
2 tablespoons pine nuts
4 cloves garlic

Place all ingredients in blender or food proces-

sor. Cover and blend on medium speed, stopping blender occasionally to scrape sides or process, until smooth.

NOTE: Freeze any remaining Pesto up to 6 months. Let stand at room temperature until thawed, at least 4 hours.

Tortellini Soup

2 cloves garlic, finely chopped
2 medium stalks celery, chopped
1 small onion, chopped
1 medium carrot, chopped
3 tablespoons butter
8 cups chicken broth
4 cups water
2 packages (10 ounces each) dried cheese-filled tortellini
2 tablespoons chopped fresh parsley
½ teaspoon pepper
1 teaspoon freshly grated nutmeg
Grated Parmesan cheese

Cover and cook garlic, celery, onion and carrot in butter in 6-quart Dutch oven over medium-low heat 10 minutes. Stir in chicken broth and water. Heat to boiling; reduce heat. Stir in tortellini; cover and simmer 20 minutes, stirring occasionally, or until tortellini are tender.

Stir in parsley, pepper and nutmeg. Cover and cook 10 minutes. Top each serving with cheese.   **8 to 10 servings**

PER SERVING: Calories 295; Protein 17 g; Carbohydrate 21 g; Fat 16 g; Cholesterol 120 mg; Sodium 1080 mg

Low-Sodium Soups & Stews

If you'd like less sodium in your soups and stews, the following is a comparison of salt and the various chicken-and-beef-broth ingredient choices you have from the supermarket and your cupboard shelves:

INGREDIENT	MILLIGRAMS OF SODIUM
1 teaspoon salt	2130
½ teaspoon salt	1065
¼ teaspoon salt	535
1 teaspoon (or 1 cube) chicken or beef bouillon	900
1 teaspoon low-sodium chicken or beef bouillon granules	5
8 ounces prepared condensed canned chicken or beef broth	750
7¼ ounces ready-to-eat-canned chicken or beef broth	910
7¼ ounces ready-to-eat canned ⅓ less salt chicken or beef broth	580
10½ ounces ready-to-eat canned low-sodium chicken or beef broth	70

Lentil Vegetable Soup

1 cup chopped onion (about 1 large)
2 teaspoons chile powder
1 teaspoon salt
1 teaspoon ground cumin
2 cloves garlic, finely chopped
1 can (6 ounces) spicy tomato juice
3 cups water
1 cup dried lentils, sorted and rinsed (about 6 ounces)
1 can (14½ ounces) whole tomatoes, undrained
1 can (4 ounces) chopped green chiles, undrained
1 cup fresh or frozen whole kernel corn
2 cups julienne strips zucchini (about 2 small)

Heat onion, chile powder, salt, cumin, garlic and tomato juice to boiling in 3-quart saucepan; reduce heat. Cover and simmer 5 minutes. Stir in remaining ingredients except corn and zucchini. Heat to boiling; reduce heat. Cover and simmer 20 minutes. Stir in corn; cover and simmer 10 minutes. Stir in zucchini; cover and simmer about 5 minutes or until lentils and zucchini are tender. **6 servings**

PER SERVING: Calories 165; Protein 11 g; Carbohydrate 32 g; Fat 1 g; Cholesterol 0 mg; Sodium 590 mg

Lentil Vegetable Soup

Lentil Stew

2 teaspoons vegetable oil
1 cup chopped onion (about 1 large)
1 clove garlic, finely chopped
2 cups coarsely chopped potatoes (about 2 medium)
1 cup dried lentils
¼ cup chopped fresh parsley
3 cups water
½ teaspoon salt
½ teaspoon ground cumin
¼ teaspoon pepper
¼ teaspoon ground mace
8 ounces small mushrooms, cut into halves
1 can (28 ounces) whole tomatoes, undrained

Heat oil in Dutch oven over medium-high heat. Cook onion and garlic in oil, stirring frequently, until onion is tender. Stir in remaining ingredients; break up tomatoes. Heat to boiling; reduce heat. Cover and simmer about 40 minutes, stirring occasionally, until potatoes are tender.

6 servings

PER SERVING: Calories 210; Protein 11 g; Carbohydrate 37 g; Fat 2 g; Cholesterol 0 mg; Sodium 400 mg

Hearty Bean and Pasta Stew

1 cup coarsely chopped tomato (about 1 large)
¾ cup uncooked shell macaroni
¼ cup chopped onion (about 1 small)
¼ cup chopped green bell pepper (about ½ small)
1 tablespoon chopped fresh or 1 teaspoon dried basil leaves
1 teaspoon Worcestershire sauce
1 clove garlic, finely chopped
1 can (16 ounces) kidney beans, drained
1 can (8 ounces) garbanzo beans, drained
1 can (14½ ounces) chicken broth

Mix all ingredients in 2-quart saucepan. Heat to boiling, stirring occasionally; reduce heat. Cover and simmer about 15 minutes, stirring occasionally, until macaroni is tender. **4 servings**

PER SERVING: Calories 350; Protein 20 g; Carbohydrate 59 g; Fat 4 g; Cholesterol 0 mg; Sodium 690 mg

Peanut Soup

Raw peanuts can be found in health food stores and Oriental groceries.

7 cups water
¾ cup skinless raw peanuts
6 medium dried black mushrooms
½ medium onion
2 small tomatoes
1 tablespoon vegetable oil
1 teaspoon salt
1 teaspoon sugar

Heat water to boiling; reduce heat. Add peanuts; cover and simmer 1½ hours. (Do not boil or broth will be cloudy.)

Soak mushrooms in hot water 20 minutes or until soft; drain. Rinse in warm water; drain.

Squeeze out excess moisture. Remove and discard stems; cut caps into ½-inch pieces. Cut onion into ½-inch pieces. Place tomatoes in boiling water; boil 1 minute. Immediately place in cold water. Remove peel and seeds; cut into ½-inch pieces.

Heat wok until very hot. Add vegetable oil; tilt wok to coat side. Add onion; stir-fry until crisp-tender. Add mushrooms and tomatoes; stir-fry 2 minutes. Stir in salt and sugar. Add vegetable mixture to peanuts and broth. Heat to boiling; reduce heat. Simmer covered 20 minutes.

6 servings

PER SERVING: Calories 150; Protein 5 g; Carbohydrate 7 g; Fat 11 g; Cholesterol 0 mg; Sodium 360 mg

Santa Fe Melon Soup (page 77)

5

Warm-Weather Soups

Cold Raspberry Soup

Because of their rich flavor, cold fruit soups are Scandinavian favorites, and no doubt this will be a hit with you as well.

4 cups fresh raspberries
½ cup sugar
¼ cup dry red wine or cranberry juice
1 cup sour cream

Place raspberries, sugar and wine in blender. Cover and blend until smooth. Stir in sour cream. Cover and refrigerate 1 to 2 hours until cold. Serve with dollops of sour cream and raspberries if desired. **4 servings**

PER SERVING: Calories 190; Protein 2 g; Carbohydrate 28 g; Fat 8 g; Cholesterol 25 mg; Sodium 15 mg

Cream of Cherry Soup

1 pound dark sweet cherries, pitted and cut into fourths
½ cup sugar
3 cups water
1 teaspoon lemon juice
¼ teaspoon ground cardamom
2 tablespoons cornstarch
2 tablespoons water
½ cup sour cream
⅓ cup dry red wine, chilled, if desired
8 whole dark sweet cherries

Heat cut-up cherries, sugar, 3 cups water, the lemon juice and cardamom to boiling. Reduce heat; simmer uncovered until cherries are tender, about 10 minutes. Pour half the cherry mixture into blender container. Cover and blend on high speed until smooth. Repeat with remaining mixture. Return to saucepan; heat to boiling. Mix cornstarch and 2 tablespoons water; stir gradually into cherries. Continue boiling, stirring constantly, until soup thickens and becomes clear, about 2 minutes. Cover and refrigerate until chilled, at least 4 hours. Just before serving, stir in sour cream and wine. Garnish each serving with whole cherry. **8 servings**

PER SERVING: Calories 115; Protein 1 g; Carbohydrate 21 g; Fat 3 g; Cholesterol 10 mg; Sodium 10 mg

Chilled Pear-Mint Soup

To cut down on chilling time, start with thoroughly chilled pears. Pears are at their most flavorful and juicy when ripe—a ripe pear yields slightly to gentle pressure.

4 ripe medium pears
1 cup half-and-half
¼ cup firmly packed mint leaves
1 tablespoon sugar
2 tablespoons lime juice

Pare and core pears. Cut into large pieces. Place pear pieces and remaining ingredients in blender or food processor. Cover and blend on high speed, or process, 3 minutes or until smooth. Refrigerate 5 hours or until chilled. Stir before serving. Garnish with mint leaves if desired. Refrigerate any remaining soup.

6 servings

PER SERVING: Calories 120; Protein 2 g; Carbohydrate 18 g; Fat 5 g; Cholesterol 15 mg; Sodium 20 mg

Fresh Fruit Soup

Pick the most luscious, appealing fruit available on the day you make this soup. Enjoy the new flavors you find when you use different fruits.

3 tablespoons sugar
3 tablespoons cornstarch
⅛ teaspoon salt
1¼ cups red wine or cranberry juice cocktail
1 cup water
1½ cups cranberry juice cocktail
3 cups fresh fruit, such as strawberries, blueberries, bananas, seedless green grapes, cantaloupe, pitted cherries

Mix sugar, cornstarch and salt in 3-quart saucepan; stir in wine and water. Heat to boiling, stirring constantly. Boil and stir 1 minute. Remove from heat; stir in cranberry juice. Cover loosely and refrigerate until chilled.

Stir in fruit. Top each serving with spoonful of sour cream or whipped cream, if desired.

9 servings

PER SERVING: Calories 85; Protein 0 g; Carbohydrate 21 g; Fat 0 g; Cholesterol 0 mg; Sodium 35 mg

Easy Fruit Soups

• Blend or process 1 package (8 ounces) cream cheese, softened, and 1 chilled 16-ounce can fruit for a quick fruit soup. Stir in additional liquid such as white wine or sparkling water, if necessary, until of desired thickness. Add cinnamon, nutmeg or allspice to taste.

• For another easy fruit soup, blend or process 1 package (16 ounces) frozen fruit without sugar and 1 package (8 ounces) cream cheese, softened. Stir in additional liquid, if necessary, until of desired thickness, and spice to taste.

Santa Fe Melon Soup

1 large cantaloupe (about 4 pounds),
    pared, seeded and chopped
3 tablespoons sugar
2 tablespoons chopped fresh mint leaves
½ cup sour cream
¼ cup dry white wine, if desired
2 teaspoons grated orange peel
Fresh mint leaves

Place cantaloupe, sugar and 2 tablespoons mint in blender or food processor; cover and blend or process until smooth. Stir in sour cream, wine and orange peel. Garnish with mint leaves.

6 servings

PER SERVING: Calories 125; Protein 2 g; Carbohydrate 20 g; Fat 4 g; Cholesterol 15 mg; Sodium 25 mg

Poppy Seed Soup

1 cup half-and-half
½ cup poppy seed
2 cups (16 ounces) vanilla yogurt
3 tablespoons honey
½ teaspoon ground nutmeg
¼ teaspoon salt

Mix half-and-half and poppy seed. Let stand 15 minutes. Place poppy seed mixture in blender or food processor. Add remaining ingredients. Cover and blend on medium speed, or process, about 3 minutes or until completely mixed. Cover and refrigerate at least 4 hours or until thoroughly chilled. **6 servings**

PER SERVING: Calories 225; Protein 6 g; Carbohydrate 17 g; Fat 11 g; Cholesterol 20 mg; Sodium 150 mg

Avocado Soup

3 cups chicken broth
1 cup half-and-half
1 tablespoon chopped onion
¾ teaspoon salt
¼ teaspoon chopped fresh cilantro
Dash of pepper
2 large avocados, cut up
1 clove garlic, crushed

Place 1½ cups of the chicken broth and the remaining ingredients in blender or food processor. Cover and blend on medium speed, or process, until smooth. Stir remaining broth into avocado mixture.

Cover and refrigerate about 2 hours or until chilled. Garnish with sour cream and paprika or avocado slices if desired. **6 servings**

PER SERVING: Calories 175; Protein 8 g; Carbohydrate 7 g; Fat 14 g; Cholesterol 15 mg; Sodium 1080 mg

Vichyssoise

Chef Louis Diat of the Ritz-Carlton in New York City created this French classic in 1910. He added milk to the traditional French hot potato soup and then chilled it. It was named Vichyssoise after the French town of Vichy, a fashionable resort.

  1 tablespoon margarine or butter
  1 medium onion, chopped (about ½ cup)
  2 medium potatoes, pared and coarsely chopped (about 2 cups)
  ½ cup chopped celery
  1 can (14½ ounces) chicken broth
  1½ cups milk
  1 cup half-and-half
  ⅛ teaspoon pepper
  ¼ teaspoon salt
  ¼ teaspoon ground nutmeg

Heat margarine in 2-quart saucepan over medium heat. Cook onion in margarine about 2 minutes. Add potatoes, celery and chicken broth. Heat to boiling; reduce heat. Cover and simmer about 15 minutes or until vegetables are tender. Place undrained mixture in blender or food processor. Cover and blend on low speed, or process, until smooth.

Stir in remaining ingredients. Refrigerate soup about 5 hours or until thoroughly chilled. Garnish with chopped fresh chives and ground nutmeg if desired. **4 servings**

MICROWAVE DIRECTIONS: Place onion and margarine in 2-quart microwavable casserole. Cover tightly and microwave on high 2 minutes. Add potatoes, celery and chicken broth. Cover tightly and microwave 8 to 10 minutes or until boiling; stir. Cover tightly and microwave 7 to 9 minutes or until vegetables are tender. Continue as directed.

PER SERVING: Calories 240; Protein 9 g; Carbohydrate 24 g; Fat 12 g; Cholesterol 30 mg; Sodium 580 mg

Summer Cold Soup

This Italian soup is very nice served with crusty bread.

  2 tablespoons olive oil
  4 roma (plum) tomatoes, chopped*
  2 cloves garlic, finely chopped
  4 slices prosciutto or fully cooked Virginia ham, cut into ¼-inch stips
  2 medium cucumbers, pared, cut into fourths and sliced
  2 cups whipping (heavy) cream
  1 cup chicken broth
  1 teaspoon pepper
  ½ teaspoon salt
  ½ cup sliced green olives
  1 green onion (with top), chopped
  4 ice cubes

Heat oil in 4-quart Dutch oven over medium-high heat. Sauté tomatoes and garlic in oil. Stir in prosciutto and cucumbers. Stir in whipping cream, chicken broth, pepper and salt.

Heat to boiling; reduce heat. Cover and simmer 40 minutes, stirring occasionally. Cover and refrigerate until chilled but no longer than 48 hours.

Ladle soup into 4 chilled individual bowls. Top each with olives, onion and ice cube.

4 servings

*4 canned Italian pear-shaped tomatoes can be substituted for the fresh tomatoes.

PER SERVING: Calories 570; Protein 12 g; Carbohydrate 15 g; Fat 51 g; Cholesterol 150 mg; Sodium 1190 mg

Summer Cold Soup

Soup Garnishes

Soup is delicious on its own, but garnishes can add special flavor and texture. Try some of these garnishes on your favorite soups:

- Lemon or lime slices or zest

- Bell pepper rings

- Sliced green onions

- Thinly sliced carrots

- Croutons

- Crackers, oyster crackers, corn chips

- Popcorn

- Sprigs of snipped parsley or dill

- Paprika

- Toasted nuts

- Shredded cheese

- Hard-cooked eggs—sliced, crumbled or chopped

- Cooked, crumbled bacon

- Sour cream, whipped cream or yogurt

Green Pea Soup

1 package (16 ounces) frozen green peas
1 cup milk
2 tablespoons margarine or butter
2 tablespoons all-purpose flour
¾ teaspoon salt
⅛ teaspoon pepper
½ cup whipping (heavy) cream or half-and-half
Mint leaves

Cook peas as directed on package; reserve ½ cup for garnish if desired. Place remaining peas and the milk in blender or food processor. Cover and blend or process until of uniform consistency.

Heat margarine in 2-quart saucepan until melted. Stir in flour, salt and pepper. Cook, stirring constantly, until smooth and bubbly. Remove from heat; stir in pea mixture. Heat to boiling, stirring constantly. Boil and stir 1 minute. Stir in whipping cream; heat just until hot (do not boil). Cover and refrigerate soup until chilled. If soup is too thick when ready to serve, stir in additional cream or half-and-half until of desired consistency. Garnish each serving with reserved peas and mint leaves if desired.   **4 servings**

PER SERVING: Calories 260; Protein 8 g; Carbohydrate 21 g; Fat 16 g; Cholesterol 40 mg; Sodium 590 mg

Green Pea Soup, Cream of Carrot Soup

Cream of Carrot Soup

1 small onion, chopped
2 tablespoons margarine or butter
6 carrots, chopped
2 tablespoons dry white wine or water
3 cups water
1 tablespoon instant chicken bouillon
1 teaspoon salt
⅛ teaspoon ground nutmeg
Dash of pepper
1 cup whipping (heavy) cream

Cook and stir onion in margarine in 2-quart saucepan over medium heat until softened. Stir in carrots and wine. Heat to boiling; reduce heat. Cover and simmer 10 minutes. Stir in water, bouillon (dry), salt, nutmeg and pepper. Heat to boiling; reduce heat. Cover and simmer until carrots are tender, about 30 minutes.

Pour half the carrot mixture into blender or food processor. Cover and blend on medium speed, or process until smooth; strain. Repeat with remaining mixture. Heat until hot. Beat whipping cream until stiff; stir into soup.

Cover and refrigerate about 5 hours or until thoroughly chilled.   **6 servings**

MICROWAVE DIRECTIONS: Place onion and margarine in 2-quart microwavable casserole. Cover tightly and microwave on high until onion is softened, 2 to 3 minutes. Stir in carrots and wine. Cover tightly and microwave until carrots are tender, 7 to 10 minutes. Spoon carrot mixture into blender or food processor; add 1 cup of the water. Cover and blend on medium speed, or process, until smooth.

Mix carrot mixture, remaining water, the bouillon (dry), salt, nutmeg and pepper in casserole. Cover tightly and microwave until hot and bubbly, 6 to 10 minutes. Beat whipping cream until stiff; stir into soup. Continue as directed above.

PER SERVING: Calories 190; Protein 2 g; Carbohydrate 10 g; Fat 16 g; Cholesterol 45 mg; Sodium 1090 mg

Tomato-Vegetable Soup with Yogurt

This soup may also be served warm— serve directly after adding yogurt.

1 can (24 ounces) tomato juice (3 cups)
¼ to ½ teaspoon ground red pepper
¼ teaspoon salt
1 bunch green onions (about 6 with tops), sliced
1 medium red or green pepper, coarsely chopped
1 medium zucchini, coarsely chopped
1 package (10 ounces) frozen whole kernel corn
1 container (18 ounces) plain yogurt

Heat all ingredients except yogurt to boiling in 4-quart Dutch oven; reduce heat. Simmer uncovered, stirring occasionally, until vegetables are crisp-tender, 7 to 8 minutes. Remove from heat; cool 5 minutes before adding yogurt to prevent curdling.

Stir yogurt into soup until smooth. Cover and refrigerate soup until chilled. Garnish with snipped cilantro or parsley if desired.

4 servings

PER SERVING: Calories 200; Protein 11 g; Carbohydrate 35 g; Fat 2 g; Cholesterol 10 mg; Sodium 890 mg

Cold Yogurt-Cucumber Soup

Nothing is more refreshing on a hot summer's day than this Middle Eastern favorite, a cool mixture of fresh cucumbers and tangy yogurt. It is the perfect make-ahead appetizer for sultry weather.

2 medium cucumbers
1½ cups plain yogurt
½ teaspoon salt
½ teaspoon chopped fresh mint leaves
   or ¼ teaspoon dried mint flakes
⅛ teaspoon white pepper

Cut 7 thin slices from 1 cucumber; reserve. Cut all remaining cucumber into ¾-inch chunks. Place half the cucumber chunks and ¼ cup of the yogurt in blender or food processor. Cover and blend on high speed, or process, until smooth.

Add remaining cucumber chunks, the salt, mint and white pepper. Cover and blend or process until smooth. Add remaining yogurt; cover and blend on low speed, or process, until smooth. Cover and refrigerate at least 1 hour. Garnish with reserved cucumber slices and fresh mint if desired. **7 servings**

PER SERVING: Calories 45; Protein 3 g; Carbohydrate 6 g; Fat 1 g; Cholesterol 5 mg; Sodium 190 mg

Gazpacho

1 can (28 ounces) whole tomatoes, undrained
1 cup finely chopped green bell peppers
1 cup finely chopped cucumbers
1 cup croutons
1 medium onion, chopped (about ½ cup)
2 tablespoons dry white wine or tomato juice
2 tablespoons olive or vegetable oil
1 tablespoon ground cumin
1 tablespoon vinegar
½ teaspoon salt
¼ teaspoon pepper

Place tomatoes, ½ cup bell peppers, ½ cup cucumbers, ½ cup croutons, ¼ cup onion and remaining ingredients in blender or food processor. Cover and blend on medium speed, or process, until smooth. Cover and refrigerate at least 1 hour. Serve remaining vegetables and croutons as accompaniments. **8 servings**

PER SERVING: Calories 90; Protein 2 g; Carbohydrate 11 g; Fat 4 g; Cholesterol 0 mg; Sodium 370 mg

Easy Borsch

1 can (16 ounces) shoestring beets, undrained
1 can (10½ ounces) condensed beef broth
1 cup shredded cabbage
2 tablespoons finely chopped onion
1 teaspoon sugar
1 teaspoon lemon juice
Sour cream

Heat beets, broth, cabbage, onion and sugar to boiling; reduce heat. Simmer uncovered 5 minutes. Stir in lemon juice. Serve hot, or refrigerate until chilled. Top each serving with spoonful of sour cream. **4 servings**

PER SERVING: Calories 75; Protein 3 g; Carbohydrate 9 g; Fat 3 g; Cholesterol 10 mg; Sodium 310 mg

METRIC CONVERSION GUIDE

U.S. UNITS	CANADIAN METRIC	AUSTRALIAN METRIC
Volume		
1/4 teaspoon	1 mL	1 ml
1/2 teaspoon	2 mL	2 ml
1 teaspoon	5 mL	5 ml
1 tablespoon	15 mL	20 ml
1/4 cup	50 mL	60 ml
1/3 cup	75 mL	80 ml
1/2 cup	125 mL	125 ml
2/3 cup	150 mL	170 ml
3/4 cup	175 mL	190 ml
1 cup	250 mL	250 ml
1 quart	1 liter	1 liter
1 1/2 quarts	1.5 liter	1.5 liter
2 quarts	2 liters	2 liters
2 1/2 quarts	2.5 liters	2.5 liters
3 quarts	3 liters	3 liters
4 quarts	4 liters	4 liters
Weight		
1 ounce	30 grams	30 grams
2 ounces	55 grams	60 grams
3 ounces	85 grams	90 grams
4 ounces (1/4 pound)	115 grams	125 grams
8 ounces (1/2 pound)	225 grams	225 grams
16 ounces (1 pound)	455 grams	500 grams
1 pound	455 grams	1/2 kilogram

Measurements		Temperatures	
Inches	Centimeters	Fahrenheit	Celsius
1	2.5	32°	0°
2	5.0	212°	100°
3	7.5	250°	120°
4	10.0	275°	140°
5	12.5	300°	150°
6	15.0	325°	160°
7	17.5	350°	180°
8	20.5	375°	190°
9	23.0	400°	200°
10	25.5	425°	220°
11	28.0	450°	230°
12	30.5	475°	240°
13	33.0	500°	260°
14	35.5		
15	38.0		

NOTE
The recipes in this cookbook have not been developed or tested using metric measures. When converting recipes to metric, some variations in quality may be noted.

INDEX

References to photos appear in italics.

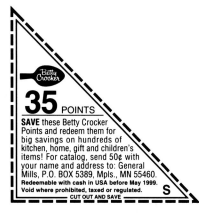